ADVANCE PRAISE

"What is the purpose of life? It isn't Jesus, Muhammad, Yahweh, or any other religious figure, self-help guru, or grand cosmic scheme to be found in the next life. As James Lindsay explains in his remarkably cogent and highly readable exposition on life and death, the meaning of life is to live, and the way to know how to live is vouchsafed to you by virtue of living. How? Read this insightful book to arrive at your own answer."

—Michael Shermer, publisher of *Skeptic* magazine and author of *The Moral Arc: How Science Makes Us Better People*

"James Lindsay and I are united by a deep commitment to live well right now. Love is a chief concern in that endeavor. We are divided over the answers to the big questions of life and our understandings of ultimately reality. Where there is no dispute is that Lindsay is one of the best writers I've read, bar none."

—Rick Henderson, Draper Campus Pastor for South Mountain Community Church in Utah

"*Life in Light of Death* is a magnificent little book about the inevitable end to our sojourns on spaceship Earth. James is a nimble writer who does a marvelous job tackling a subject that's inherently difficult to discuss. The book is eloquent, thoughtful, and a genuine pleasure to read—I highly recommend it!"

—Phil Torres, author of *The End: What Science and Religion Tell Us About the Apocalypse* and founding director of the X-Risks Institute

"Everyone we love will die and be forgotten forever, including us. In this compelling booklet Lindsay argues we can love deeper and live better once we accept this fact. Christians often say their faith leads them to love and life, but Lindsay shows another way: by accepting the truth about death. This is a very important message that should be heeded by everyone!"

—John W. Loftus, author of *Why I Became an Atheist: A Former Preacher Rejects Christianity*

"This book challenged me, a person who thought he was on good terms with death. Life in Light of Death confronts with unflinching honesty life's most irrefutable truth: we all die. James shows the way our instinctual fear of death affects our daily life for the worse and shows a surprising way forward—to live a good life, we must accept that we will die."

—Mike McHargue, author of *Finding God in the Waves* and host of *Ask Science Mike* and cohost of *The Liturgists Podcast*

LIFE
IN LIGHT OF
DEATH

James A. Lindsay

PITCHSTONE PUBLISHING
Durham, North Carolina

Pitchstone Publishing
Durham, North Carolina 27705

To contact the publisher,
please email info@pitchstonepublishing.com

Library of Congress Cataloging-in-Publication Data

Names: Lindsay, James A., author.
Title: Life in light of death / James A. Lindsay.
Description: Durham, North Carolina : Pitchstone Publishing, 2016.
Identifiers: LCCN 2016035354 (print) | LCCN 2016035647 (ebook) | ISBN
   9781634310864 (pbk. : alk. paper) | ISBN 9781634310871 (mobi) | ISBN
   9781634310888 (epub) | ISBN 9781634310895 (epdf)
Subjects: LCSH: Death. | Life.
Classification: LCC BD444 .L494 2016 (print) | LCC BD444 (ebook) | DDC
   128/.5—dc23
LC record available at https://lccn.loc.gov/2016035354

To my parents, who will die,
and
To my children, who will die as well,
and
To Emma McCarter, who never dreamed
she'd
be remembered this way
and
never will.

The flight of years began, have laid them down
In their last sleep—the dead reign there alone.
So shalt thou rest, and what if thou withdraw
In silence from the living, and no friend
Take note of thy departure? All that breathe
Will share thy destiny. The gay will laugh
When thou art gone, the solemn brood of care
Plod on, and each one as before will chase
His favorite phantom; yet all these shall leave
Their mirth and their employments, and shall come
And make their bed with thee. As the long train
Of ages glide away, the sons of men,
The youth in life's green spring, and he who goes
In the full strength of years, matron and maid,
The speechless babe, and the gray-headed man—
Shall one by one be gathered to thy side,
By those, who in their turn shall follow them.

So live, that when thy summons comes to join
The innumerable caravan, which moves
To that mysterious realm, where each shall take

His chamber in the silent halls of death,
Thou go not, like the quarry-slave at night,
Scourged to his dungeon, but, sustained and soothed
By an unfaltering trust, approach thy grave,
Like one who wraps the drapery of his couch
About him, and lies down to pleasant dreams.

—From "Thanatopsis," William Cullen Bryant (1794–1878)

CONTENTS

AUTHOR'S NOTE

This book could start dramatically. It could, from the first paragraph, shake you to your existential core, and before you're done with it, it may. It should not begin that way, though, because if it did, it would work against its goal.

Hundreds of studies have confirmed that human psychology possesses at least one vulnerability so delicate that even hearing about it will inadvertently produce its effects, changing how you think and, more importantly, what you will believe. It has the power to make you more religious, more set in your thinking and judgmental, crueler to those you perceive to be wrongdoers, more eager for fame, more likely to objectify other people and yourself, more narrow-minded and intolerant, or, on the other hand, more charitable, more interested in having children (and naming them after yourself), and more helpful. It can also make you more gullible.

Only one subject could have such power over human thought and behavior that its mere mention could change your demeanor in such dramatic ways. That subject is death, and being reminded that we will die biases us toward accepting almost any idea that lets us believe otherwise. Many psychologists are devoted to understanding this bias, which arises from what they call "mortality salience," and their approaches include terror management theory and emotional priority theory.

Most of us live in terror of death, but we can think about death in a completely different way. Our innate fear of our own mortality misleads us. The subconscious drive to manage terror creates a bias that makes us more open to certain kinds of beliefs and more closed to others. We can use this bias to our advantage, however, so that we can use death as a way to think meaningfully about life and what matters most in it. Death shouldn't horrify us; it should remind us *how* to live. This book that seems to be about death, then, is about life. It is a short exploration on the sweetness available to every person and the importance of the opportunity that life offers. Death just provides the view.

That tells you what this book is, and here is what it isn't. This is not a book about grief or grief counseling. This is not a book about working with the dying or recovering from the death of a loved one. This is not a book about specifically how you can learn to cope with a death or death in general, and so it certainly isn't a book that offers coping strategies. It doesn't aim to tell you how to do anything, in fact. Those details are left up to you because only you live your life. This is also not an academic book, not strictly speaking. It is more of a philosophical narrative, and its singular goal is to impress upon you, the reader, that you too will die and that all there is to do about it is to accept the fact of it and live as fully as possible in the meantime. Oh, and it tells you the meaning of life, in case you were wondering about that.

YOU ARE GOING TO DIE

To the dumb question "Why me?"
the cosmos barely bothers to return the reply: why not?

—Christopher Hitchens, in *Mortality*

If you want to be happy, you must accept that you will die. And so will your loved ones. Yes, you and those you love will die. You each will end interminably and eventually be forgotten, and happiness in life demands realizing this fact.

Realizing that you will die will not immediately make you happy. Quite the contrary. To find happiness in the shadow of death requires reckoning with it bravely and fiercely until the full light of life shines through. This light remains obscured until you know what death means for your life and the lives of those you love.

Everything that matters becomes much more clear once you apprehend the facts of mortality. Truly knowing that you are

13

going to die teaches what may be life's most valuable lessons: life is short, some misery is guaranteed, and yet happiness, contentment, and fulfillment are possible. The clear conclusion that follows is that seizing happiness—and helping others to do so too—while we have the chance may be the only thing that makes sense to do with our time. So, the first thing to do is acknowledge is that you are going to die.

Contemplating the brevity of life creates gratitude and a unique opportunity to live more fully. In fact, very little offers the opportunity to see life's potential like death. Contemplating death is looking into a mirror, and it allows us to see our lives differently, in ways as if for the first time. What stands out in death's reflection of life is what matters most. By seeing plainly where we will find meaning in our lives, we have the opportunity to live for it, which is to say *to really live*.

MEETING DEATH

If you meet Death upon the road, tell him your dreams.

You probably know you are going to die—sort of. I always did, and always sort of. Sort of knowing you are going to die is the way of things. It's how we live. We often believe it's what lets us keep our heads up, just in order to live, to "keep on keepin' on," as the old Len Chandler song runs. Somewhere back there, in the back of our minds, we all know we're going to die—sort of. We just don't think about it.

It's easier at first. Children are mostly free of the terror of death, and adults are nearly universally bound by its encumbrance. The terror of death creeps, coming on slowly as we grow toward adulthood.

Early in our lives, we tend to be detached from death mainly just because we are young. As children, we are unlikely to have seen much death, if any, and we have no comprehension of degeneration. Everything in childhood is omnipotent, perfect, and eternal—because why shouldn't it be? From the perspective of a child, everything always just has been. Children simply haven't lived long enough to have witnessed the kinds of changes that drive home just how temporary our existence will be. When we are young, if we think about dying at all, we do so with it remote, literally a lifetime away.

Religion, often learned in childhood, also often helps deflect our thoughts about death, even if we aren't devout. For my own part, I grew up vaguely Catholic, with even vaguer notions of Heaven and how to get there (I don't recall there being any requirements, except staying in the Church). So, even if I did consider death as a child, I never thought deeply about it. I knew I was going to die, sort of, but the idea rarely occupied my thoughts. The nature of the afterlife interested me about as much as it might any curious child, but Heaven seemed so certain and easy that it was irrelevant.

For most young adults, not much changes, except that we maintain our comfortable distance from and dismissal of death less easily. As we begin to think more abstractly, we also begin to realize the limits to our existence. We tend to encounter this realization before we have a name for it, and it takes on the form of a growing awareness of one of the many uncomfortable background noises of maturity. That nagging sense is the *terror of death*, and with it comes *existential dread*.

Because we tend to refuse to face death, the terror of death and existential dread are, like our mortality, among those things that we usually realize only "sort of." We keep them out of sight as much as possible, but they're always present, like the buzzing of so many corpse flies waiting impatiently for us, their disconsolate swarming seeming not so much around our heads as inside the dimmer rooms within it. The terror of death arises when our desire to live clashes against the realization that death is inevitable. Existential dread is the anxiety that follows when it occurs to us that our inevitable deaths threaten to erase meaning from our lives.

In each of us, terror of death eventually awakens, and once it does, it becomes impossible to go back to that blissful aspect of childhood. Once the terror of death creeps upon a person, she will never again enjoy the complete irrelevance of death. This change—the introduction to the terror of death—is an almost universal part of growing up, and learning to manage it is a significant developmental challenge as we mature.

For many, even in childhood, religion is the "answer" to these problems because it makes their resolution seem obvious. When we die, the story goes, we will go to Heaven. That belief helps because it lets profound horrors feel accounted for. Even for those who aren't particularly devout, even vague religious beliefs are sufficient to make death seem unimportant and its terror unnecessary. Religion does that. It keeps death abstract and therefore unreal, and it goes further, fundamentally denying the finality of death. That function is so central to religion, say psychologists, that it may be the very point of faith. Whether or not Marx was right to call religion "the opium of the people," its effects on the terror of death and existential dread are certainly palliative.

For me, it didn't last. I left my faith. The hymns of Heaven stopped playing and could no longer drown out the corpse flies' unendurable buzz. I had to find new ways to keep on keepin' on—and did, like most people do whether they lose their faiths or not. I didn't replace beliefs of Heaven with new beliefs of similar kind, but I kept myself distracted just with the treadmill of living. Still, I sort of knew I was going to die. *Just* sort of.

If you'll forgive the indulgence, I think my own story of coming to face death can be instructive. Had I known about what psychologists call terror management theory, which suggests that we manage the terror of death by creating symbolic systems to give life meaning, I might have recognized the ways in which I was keeping myself distracted. Embracing distractions from the terror of death is common whether people are religious or not. Mostly, I kept myself busy with life and I moralized, exactly as terror management theory predicts we will when confronted with mortality. Religion is only one way to moralize. We can moralize about politics, diet, culture, or any number of topics—nearly anything to which we can attach words like "good," "bad," "fair," "unfair," "sacred," "evil," "clean," "dirty," "uplifting," "disgusting," "pure," and "corrupt."

Once I fully realized that I would die, moralizing lost its thrill—and much of its satisfaction. Maybe self-righteousness is what we lose when we give up on Heaven. Heaven, though, is just a belief in an otherworldly Utopia, and we can believe in a vision of a perfect world too, "God's Kingdom," to be built here on Earth while we yet live by demanding moral perfection. Maybe beliefs in Utopia lure us away from an honest appraisal of just how little we know for certain about human flourishing, which is the ultimate basis of all of our moral thinking.

The full realization of my own death, to let you know, was only remarkable only in being unremarkable, something I'm quite glad for. Dramatic brushes with death aren't great to live through. All I had done to bring death into view was plan my first trip to Asia.

Up to that point, I had always been a nervous traveler, and something about the trip convinced a corner of my brain to panic at two thirty in the morning, just a few hours after booking my flight. *What if my flight goes down? It goes over the North Pole. I can't survive in the Arctic!* I couldn't shake visions of the movie *Alive*, in which a plane crash strands a soccer team on a remote and icy Andean mountain in Argentina, and the Arctic had to be much worse (if I could even survive the catastrophic crash of a Boeing 777 into a frozen ocean, that is). *What had I done?!*

My rational mind, trained as it is in statistics, spoke back calmly, *big planes almost never go down, there's nothing to worry about. Go back to sleep.* Panic doesn't always speak the language of reason, though, and it gave a convincing enough rebuttal to keep me awake. *Sometimes they do. That means that boarding that flight slightly increases your chances of dying over just staying home—with your family, who will probably survive even if you don't.* One downside to being thoroughly trained in mathematical reasoning is that even the least rational parts of your brain can use calculated logic against you.

That was it. That night, I realized the full fact of my mortality, and this time *not* sort of. *I am going to die.* Weirdly, it wasn't the fact of my coming doom that got my attention. It was the implications it had for others.

In that momentary fear of death, the kind of which I had met on occasion, the discordant melody of those ever-persistent corpse flies grew too loud for sleep. I had considered death before, sometimes quite seriously, but something was different this time. In the near pitch darkness of my bedroom, I stared at the dim silhouette of my wife's back while she lay there snoring gently beside me, and the full reality of death came upon me so heavily that I could do nothing else. The flies' wicked song was true terror of death. *I am going to die, but worse, when I do, I'll be leaving her, forever.* That thought brought a reciprocal dread: *she is going to die too, and maybe even before I will.*

Existential horror, as it works out, can become very disturbing. That night, I lay there staring at her pondering until morning, but it was only the first night. I didn't sleep fully through another night for almost a year, even after surviving my trip to Asia, and I spent most of those long, dark hours contemplating human mortality and its consequences. Before the sun rose that morning, I had realized that in all likelihood either my wife or I would die before the other, with the odds tipped ever so slightly in my favor. More than that, I realized that the luckier one won't live to tell the tale. This is how love and the reality of death are connected, and it is absolutely bitter.

It's interesting to lie there, realizing that you will die, and knowing clearly that for yourself it doesn't matter enough to be concerned with it. You'll have died, after all. Psychologists might call it "intellectualization," a defense mechanism that separates us from the emotional horror contained within the thought, but it's still an interesting place for a mind to go. It's more interesting, however, to lie there and realize what makes it matter. We live to love and to be beloved; that's why it matters. The pang and pall of mortality are far less for what we will miss than for who will be missing us.

Maybe it isn't surprising that your own death isn't the problem. Maybe it's too much, or too hard, or too remote to contemplate your own death seriously enough to meet it. You're always alive, so long as the idea called "you" makes sense.

Perhaps because of that fact, the idea of my own death has always seemed relatively easy to resign myself to, beyond the clear instinct to live. It has always seemed clear that absent certain horrors I could face my own death bravely, stoically, even, and that I probably will when I come to that point. Once it's done, after all, I won't exist to be bothered by it any longer. By dying, I get to be the only person who cares about me and doesn't have to live with my death.

Death's cheat is not provided to the lives that will continue after you die, especially the lives of those you love as much as life itself. Chances are that when you die, those you love will not, and it will be their grief—not yours—to go on living after your death. My intermittent struggle now, for instance, is not the realization that I will die one day. That I have come to terms with. It's the reality that I could die *any* day, leaving friends and family who depend on me for love and support and saddling them with the burden of grief as I go. I don't want that to happen to them far more than anything that could befall myself. Death marks an escape for ourselves and agonizing heartbreak for those we care most about. That pain is what really gets to you like nothing else can when you think about death.

Death, when you first meet him, doesn't come off as a friendly fellow.

EXISTENTIAL HORROR

I met a traveller from an antique land,
Who said—"Two vast and trunkless legs of stone
Stand in the desert. . . . Near them, on the sand,
Half sunk a shattered visage lies, whose frown,
And wrinkled lip, and sneer of cold command,
Tell that its sculptor well those passions read
Which yet survive, stamped on these lifeless things,
The hand that mocked them, and the heart that fed;
And on the pedestal, these words appear:
My name is Ozymandias, King of Kings;
Look on my Works, ye Mighty, and despair!
Nothing beside remains. Round the decay
Of that colossal Wreck, boundless and bare
The lone and level sands stretch far away."

—Percy Bysshe Shelley, "Ozymandias"

In his mythological account of Middle Earth, J. R. R. Tolkien referred to death as the "Gift of Men." To illustrate how death could be a "gift," Tolkien contrasted mankind against a fantastical race of elves who do not die. Tolkien's elves were thereby doomed to grow—and persist—bound up with the world and thus to slowly grow weary and sad within it, a fate not shared by humanity. Though men in Tolkien's account rarely welcome their "gift," he was on to something. Tolkien used his myth to paint death as a kind of sad freedom from the weariness, the sorrow, and the grinding miseries of being bound up with the world until its final end.

If we live long enough, we will come to a point in our lives when, even if we do not wish for it, we will welcome Death like a long-awaited friend. The slings and arrows of mundane fortune will gradually take their tolls, even if we are lucky enough to be spared the worst insults of advancing age. Treating death as a kind of long, final rest resonates against the toils of our lives. In that metaphor, death becomes a bittersweet reward for our struggles, the consolation prize that surely waits in case Heaven does not.

It isn't the prospect of dying that will eat away at you in the end, nor is it the fact that you will endure hardship while you live. It's that everyone you care about, if you live long enough, will die ahead of you. The loss of so many relationships, and thus of the best parts of ourselves, may be the real difficulty of aging. Even if our bodies remain spry and our minds clear and crisp, even if we succeed in remaining relevant to younger generations as we fade into the long winters of our lives, still, to live long enough is to witness our loved ones make their own ways out of being. In no small part due to Kenny Rogers and Dolly Parton, it has become cliché, but the truth is enduring: you really can't make old friends.

The difficulty of loss is partly that we lose the connections we share with those we love—their companionship, what they can offer us, the comforts they bring us, and memories they awake. Our own identities are wrapped up in our closest relationships, and as we lose them we also lose parts of ourselves. We are who we are to others, especially those we care most about. We are made of our support systems. We are our communities. Except in rare cases, no amount of individualism or love for our activities can overcome the fact that we are "ultrasocial" animals with psychologies evolved in service to that fact. We need each other partly because we are each other, and that's why the real tragedy of death is that we all must go eventually. Our own demise marks the end of having to endure grief alongside our joy, but it also marks the passing of that torch to those who, in their turns, love us.

While death may be a grim mercy, it isn't a reward. Death is not a glorious affair. In fact, death would be immensely boring if it possessed the capacity to be anything at all. It is tempting to pull upon the usual descriptions, that death is empty, that it is nothingness, that it is a long rest, but these are all wrong. Death is the termination of being, and in that, it arrives and then simply isn't. Some measure of the terror of death comes from the discomfort of imagining what cannot be imagined: not existing.

That we die is just the beginning of existential dread. Think for a moment. You can probably name all of your grandparents. How many of your great-grandparents can you name? You have eight of them. And how many of their sixteen parents can you name? And just how many generations back do you have to go before you cannot name a single person in that tier of your family tree? Even if you have studied your own genealogy thoroughly, the integer you must have in mind is not a very large one. Except in rare exceptions, it's unlikely you need all ten of your fingers to count them. In most cases, it isn't even five, and they're *your* ancestors.

Even if you know something of your ancestors who lived and died before you were born, you can't be said to remember *them*. You may know their names, have seen pictures of them, or recall a few stories, but you don't know them and never did. You don't know their favorite foods; you don't know their hobbies; you don't know the minds that made them, *them*. Their legacy is literally your entire life, but you do not and cannot know much of anything about them. So the fact of mortality isn't just that you'll die. You'll be forgotten too.

This moment is when the mind, set upon itself and its fundamental incompatibility with nonexistence, starts casting wildly for counterexamples. What about Isaac Newton? That was four hundred years ago, and he hasn't been forgotten! What about Pontius Pilate? That's two thousand years ago, and he's remembered in remarkable (and probably unfair) infamy! Socrates, Epicurus, Buddha, Lao Tzu, and Confucius were a few hundred years before that. And we don't remember only men; there were Cleopatra, Helen of Troy, Zenobia of Palmyra, and Queen Amyitis, all great women of antiquity. History is littered with exceptions: names of people who haven't been forgotten. You can probably name a hundred exceptions . . . from amongst many billions who are nothing more to any of us than a bland quantitative fact about the history of our species.

That's the thing. They are exceptions, and they are history. The statistical potency behind the fact that you will be forgotten is immensely strong, and the grinding logic of reality is stronger. Even should you make the books, what we remember of historical figures is remarkably selective and filled with legend, and none of them now are the people themselves. In becoming history they became immaterial things, just names, ideas, and stories.

It gets worse. Not only do the terror of death and existential dread hang grotesquely on mortality or being irretrievably forgotten; none of that hits home quite so hard as realizing that extinction will be universal. Memory itself will one day cease, and all of the efforts of all living beings will be milled down by time to a purposeless grist. Along with every detail of human history, even the greatest and most notorious characters will all be forgotten eventually, as will even the most dazzling and lurid names to come.

The final termination of humanity, and even of conscious awareness itself, takes some explaining. These are notions so alien to human experience that the mind, even in grasping their inevitability, seems to reject them automatically as unreal. They also threaten a kind of existential dread so overwhelming that it threatens to destroy all of our grandiose illusions of immortality. Then again, no other consideration possesses so much power to bring life's purposes home to us. For these reasons, the long, lifeless fate of the universe and humanity's eventual fall are well worth investigating.

Who can dare to guess at how long humanity, including its evolutionary descendants, has left as a species in our vast cosmos? There are some reasons to doubt whether the show will last another fifty years, like the perilous combination of our apish bent toward bellicose tribalism and the availability of weapons of mass destruction. Another would be our unwillingness to take steps to stabilize our environment, including atmospheric levels of carbon dioxide and other greenhouse gases. Another is that we largely ignore these kinds of existential threats in much the same way we ignore our own inevitable deaths. We are utterly dependent upon the earth and have no viable backup plan in the event of global catastrophe—and for hardly any better reason than "why would we?"

On the other hand, our gritty penchant for survival suggests our descendants may still have millions of years to go. The great show called humanity—or the greater one called life—will only last until it doesn't, though, and the end is certain.

Whether soon or not, once we go, not much of what we have done will last. Earth is not a nostalgic place without humans around to maintain the feeling. Nature will quickly reclaim what we have tamed, and it will leave most of our proudest triumphs in broken ruins. I once saw a stunning picture of an abandoned village in China that had been completely reclaimed by lush vegetation. It looks like a piece of art depicting some combination of buildings and ruins escaping up the side of a mountain but rendered completely in vivid green mosses, trees, and ivies. The entire village had been reclaimed by the jungle in a mere matter of a few years. Now think: hardly a recognizable trace of humanity's great exploits would survive a single geological epoch.

The harder fact is, even if we succeed in stabilizing our temperaments and our environment for ourselves, Earth cannot stay our home indefinitely. For one thing, our planet isn't perfectly safe from existential catastrophes. Earth is vulnerable to impactors from space like large asteroids or comets, which have caused mass extinctions before and may again. Our home planet is also geologically active, a cooling ball of metal and rock with a delicate miles-thin crust that occasionally produces volcanic and supervolcanic activity that could drive humanity to extinction. It is difficult to imagine such threats being as real as they are, but it is thought that the Yellowstone Caldera in the Western United States harbors the potential for such an explosion.

And then there's the Sun. In about 5.4 billion years, the Sun will swell to an immense red giant star. When that happens, Earth (along with Mercury and Venus) will be destroyed, and Mars may be as well. The Sun itself will grow so large as to swallow them, and they—and everything on them—will be vaporized in nuclear plasma.

Long before that, however, the Sun will render life unlivable unless we devise some technological miracle beyond our current imagination. After about another billion years, the Sun's slowly increasing radiance will become intense enough to destroy any possibility of life on Earth. Under that unbearable daylight a runaway greenhouse effect will render Earth completely uninhabitable. Within 3.5 billion years, the increased radiance of the Sun and runaway greenhouse effect will heat our oceans to boiling, and all of the water vapor on Earth will escape into space. The planet will become a completely uninhabitable wasteland, a dry Venus, unless we can somehow move the orbit of Earth further from the Sun. The Cosmos will afford no pity for any population on Earth; all remaining life will die, then all will be destroyed, and then at long whiles all will be consumed.

There are other places to live in the Solar System, but should we find a way to expand Earth's orbit or escape to Mars or the moons of outer planets like Jupiter and Saturn, we'll face solar calamity anyway. Even should humanity manage to survive somewhere in our Solar System under a dramatically pulsating red giant Sun, our children's long-descended children will have the Sun's death to contend with as well. The Sun, less than six billion years from now, will run short of nuclear fuel and cease to be a red giant. Then, it will form a planetary nebula by shedding most of its atmosphere as it collapses to a white dwarf. The planets will not survive this process, or at least no living thing on them will. Hot ionized gas streaming away from the Sun—much of its matter—will sterilize most of what's left of the Solar System.

Human ingenuity runs deeply, however, and it will run more deeply as technology comes to the assist in years to come. We may be able to devise a shield against the Sun's last gasp, but then we'd find ourselves in a worse predicament. What would remain of the Sun would not put out nearly enough energy to support life on any surface that would remain in the Solar System, and our remaining options would become very difficult. For humanity to outlive the Sun, we will have to leave Earth, and we may have to leave our Solar System entirely.

Because we have such a hard time accepting death, casually considering our escape from Earth's destruction may make success seem inevitable, or at least hopefully plausible. Pause and appreciate the realistic side of an ambition to leave our home world, though. Getting away from Earth will be hard. We currently struggle to keep a handful of highly trained humans alive in space for just months at a time, and a human exodus project would require managing all of the necessities—and messiness—of life for millions, if not billions of everyday citizens, for untold numbers of generations. Our science fiction, our will to live, and the inconceivability of our eventual extinction lead us to believe that such endeavors will be easier than they really will be.

Our easiest lifeboats would be technological challenges at the very reaches of today's imagination: generational ships upon which generations of humans can live out their entire lives. Building them, most likely in orbit, would be unfathomably difficult and expensive, and getting people by the millions onto them would be far harder. If we could achieve the feat, these will still be but high-tech dinghies adrift upon the most perilous and vast oceans imaginable. Few environments are more hostile to human survival than space.

Large ships that could manage their distance to the Sun carefully would make for our most obvious chance, so long as the energy lasts. Other easier possibilities exist, like devising interstellar incubators, such as ships equipped only with robots and the necessary genetic material and equipment to reconstitute human life when a suitable new home-world could be reached. The next step would be a desperate flight still. Our lifeboats would eventually need to be brought to other planetary systems temporarily made habitable by the brief grace of another star.

Getting to another suitable star will not be easy. Everything needed for generational ships in orbit around the Sun would be needed, and more, to take one to another star. To make it to another star system, even generational ships traveling at very high speeds would need a safe, reliable power source that could enable a journey potentially lasting centuries while sustaining a microcosm of human civilization. There would be no Sun to draw upon in interstellar space, and failure would turn them into humanity's last great catacombs. Alternatives, like incubator ships, would require far less to keep them afloat, but they still would carry what will eventually prove to be humanity's entire hope for survival on a very difficult mission.

Let's be optimistic. Upon arrival at a new planetary home, should we ever get there, colonizing it would be yet another immensely difficult project. The planet would have to be able to support human life or made to be, either by forming enclosed artificial habitats or by modifying an entire global system. People would have to be delivered safely into those environments and protected from them against unknown dangers and, if the planet already supports any life, diseases. It's not clear that these hopes are even possible, even with the technological advances that millions of productive years might bring. Even technology cannot outwit the laws of physics, and on the scales involved in interstellar travel, physics might win the game against us.

Even should we manage it, to navigate all of these incredible perils is still only to buy our descendants a bit more time. In the shorter term, maybe a few more billion years, the great interstellar exoduses would have to be repeated. Like all people, all stars eventually die.

Amidst this sea of troubles is Andromeda. The Andromeda Galaxy is coming, and in about four billion years it will collide with the Milky Way. Galaxies are relatively diffuse objects, and so their collisions aren't quite the cataclysms that we might imagine. Instead, they are vast engines of star formation and disruption of stable patterns of stellar motion, and so the collision of Andromeda with the Milky Way will still present enormous potential threats to any life around to see it. As we are very unlikely ever to escape our home galaxy, with the arrival of Andromeda, humanity's chances of survival diminish further.

Then, for all our valiance, in the end there is no way out. At some point should human descendants repeatedly manage to make the near-impossible feat of star system recolonization routine and persist long enough, they would run out of star systems to colonize. The long, slow end—death beyond any hope—is coming. The gears of entropy grind in only one direction, and it isn't the one that supports life interminably.

The universe is physically different because we have lived, but poetic pretense amounts to nothing more than hopeful feelings tinged with vanity. The material universe isn't equipped to remember you or to care that you hope to be remembered. It may seem dismal, but you will die; you will be forgotten; and in the long run, nothing of anything you ever do will remain.

Death and extinction, with their inevitability and interminable indifference, are two of the hard facts of living. Even now you may find your mind desperately fighting it, trying to reject the finality of what you just read. We have a hard time admitting the truth. We will die, as will everyone else, and eventually all of our greatest works will slip from memory. We are all Ozymandias in our own ways, and so upon our own works we look, and we despair. That despair we call existential dread.

Even without being informed on the science, the author of Ecclesiastes surely contemplated similar points, and they threatened to make a nihilist of him. "Everything is vanity!" he wrote, and the dread of it turned him to religion so he might deny it. The universe must care! There must be meaning! Proud and defiant humans demand it because we are scared to die and to be made meaningless by death! Therefore man invented God and made him the great figurehead of our most earnest death-denying projects: morality and religion.

That everything is vanity can be altogether easy to believe even though it's wrong. It happens precisely when we forget we are human. It happens when we refuse to recognize that we have no choice but to die—and thus that nothing makes sense but to live before death takes you in your turn.

Termination and irrelevance are the two great horrors of death and extinction, and for them, the only potential remedies are perspective and pretense. We can achieve perspective and thereby eschew pretense by facing death honestly. In that way, many of our greatest torments are avoidable. *Emotional priority theory*, a partial rival to terror management theory, gives us some idea about how we can avoid those miseries. It tells us that we can answer the terror of death by focusing our attention on our most important emotions while we live. Our focus in examining death, then, should lie less on death and more on life, love, relationship, and happiness. Death is but a mirror into which we will stare so that we can see those blessings more clearly.

THE EMERGENCY

*Now most of us do our best to not think about death,
but there's always part of our minds that knows this can't
go on forever. Part of us always knows that we're just a
doctor's visit away or a phone call away from being starkly
reminded with the fact of our own mortality, or of those
closest to us. Now I'm sure many of you in this room
have experienced this in some form. You must know how
uncanny it is to suddenly be thrown out of the normal
course of your life and just be given the full-time job of
not dying, or of caring for someone who is.*

—Sam Harris, from "Death and the Present Moment"

To contemplate death requires enduring the terror it brings
upon us. Before continuing, if reading about the bleak facts
of extinction did not cause you to feel true terror of death
and existential dread—and if you believe yourself to be

psychologically equipped to face them—invite yourself into those feelings now. For the moment, you need only let them make you slightly uncomfortable.

If you still need help getting there, just pause for a moment to notice that someday, nearly everyone gets *that* phone call about someone they love. Yes, *that* one. Imagine getting it now, setting this book aside to answer the worst phone call of your life.

These dreadful feelings that arise peel back the pretense enough to see things differently. It stares reality in the face, and, like a mirror, reflects back to us the meaning in our lives. Typically banal questions like "what do I want out of life?" and "what really matters?" suddenly take on the immediacy and urgency of a house fire.

In a house fire, you have two choices: you can stay put, whether dreading or ignoring the flames, and burn, or you can get out. With the terror of death, it seems that the only way out of *this* fire is through it—by contemplating the reality of your life in light of its certain conclusion. A few minutes a day can suffice, but, chances are, you're pretty far behind.

Both this immediacy and this urgency of the need to live while we have the chance are multiplied when we think not of ourselves dying, but of our closest loved ones who live on after our death. Take a moment to imagine yourself making videos for your closest family and friends—your partners, your children, your parents—to find as a last keepsake should you die before they do. These could be just you talking to the camera about life, about them, and about what they mean to you, or they could be elaborate productions in which you share things with them you never want them to forget, things you love in a way that you want to have illuminate their lives like they illuminate yours.

What would you say? What would you show? What of yourself would you give to those videos? And what would you give to have even the simplest one from a close loved one you've already lost in some untimely way, now that you can't get one?

We live much of our lives, it has been said, merely waiting for the future to arrive with its potential for happiness, and it never does. Eventually, a day is coming after which no future can arrive. That day will be your last. Immeasurably worse than its eventuality, this is a truth we fear too much to face. We deny it, willfully forgetting, actively fleeing, and blindly overlooking the plainest truth about our future, among other behaviors more contemptible. Many of us also spend much of our lives moralizing, browbeating, manipulating, and hating others in the cruel service of denial. Thus horror of death often begets horror in life.

DENYING DEATH

The prospect of death, Dr. Johnson said, wonderfully concentrates the mind. The main thesis of this book is that it does much more than that: the idea of death, the fear of it, haunts the human animal like nothing else; it is a mainspring of human activity—activity designed largely to avoid the fatality of death, to overcome it by denying in some way that it is the final destiny for man.

—The first two sentences of Ernest Becker's
The Denial of Death

It may be that the greatest of humanity's preoccupations is the denial of death. Our desperation to deny death is so strong that a number of other high-minded denials orbit around it. Humans deny that we are animals partly because animals die. We deny human nature for the same reason. We deny that we *are* bodies by insisting that we have them instead, creating distance between our mortality and the immortal minds we feel ourselves to be. We deny science that conflicts with our views of immortality or that reminds us of our certain doom. We deny the need to look at death honestly, and we even deny that we are denying death.

We construct no more elaborate psychological labyrinths for ourselves than those we might call "immortality projects," as Ernest Becker did in his strange but landmark 1973 Pulitzer Prize–winning book, *The Denial of Death*, upon which terror management theory is based. We deny death in overt ways and also in very subtle ways. Some of the ways we deny death, like moral adherence, don't even feel like denial. Becker, though he may have been overreaching, insisted we take *nothing* in life as seriously as the denial of death, and that there is no other way to live but to go on denying it. Not only do we construct these elaborate labyrinths, then; we reliably lose ourselves in them and consistently fail to realize that we're lost.

At the heart of our immortality projects are immortality stories, narratives we tell ourselves to pretend we can defeat death. An enduring facet of human psychology is that we have a strong tendency to embrace immortality narratives whenever we are reminded of death, and, according to English philosopher Stephen Cave, they tend to follow four major themes. These are physical immortality stories in which we seek ways to live forever, resurrection stories in which we return from death, transcendence stories in which death doesn't matter, and legacy stories in which we redefine immortality in a less literal way.

There is an alternative. We can write an immortality story with a different theme: *mortality*. We're going to die. That's it. What should we do about it? *We defeat death by living while we have the chance.*

This alternative is the tale of the philosophical movement

called *existentialism*, but we needn't follow the existentialists into their jejune adoption of meaninglessness. Meaning is entirely behind our eyes, and it is immediately in front of our noses, especially when we're kissing someone we love. We'll come back to this idea, and when we do we won't make the existentialists' mistake.

First, to become more familiar with the immortality stories we're naturally prone to, so that we might learn to avoid them, let's explore the four categories in more detail.

The simplest immortality stories that we tell ourselves merely express a desire to extend physical life indefinitely. This theme has been a constant thread of false hope and disturbing experimentation throughout human history. Alchemists experimented with heavy metals to concoct elixirs of enduring life. Pope Innocent VIII tried blood, famously attempting to renew his own youth by receiving transfusions from young boys. In the twentieth century, we turned to hormones, thinking that hormone therapies may prove a fountain of youth. Today we hope for gene therapies and, for the sake of humanity, a way off our home planet. Death doesn't care. It awaits nonetheless.

There is, of course, nothing intrinsically wrong with hoping to extend life, but as an immortality project, it can easily begin to miss its own point. A long, miserable life is no consolation. Living longer but with a poor quality of life doesn't just fail the colloquial notion of *living*; it's a kind of torture we routinely inflict upon ourselves in the vain pursuit of impossible immortality.

Amazingly, the bald fear of death often drives us to undergo risky, expensive medical procedures near the end of life, even when we know that our situation is ultimately hopeless. Sometimes, merely in order not to die quite yet, we take a risk that is at best a chance at a little bit longer and at worst the promise of persisting—in agony or having lost our minds. The truth is, there will come a point at which we simply are dying, and life-saving interventions at that point are little more than ghastly efforts to extend life's quantity without regard for its quality. A lesson we can draw from our fervor in the practice of hopeless end-of-life medicine is that the psychological torment of the terror of death must at least slightly outweigh both the drawn-out pain of a pointlessly slow and agonizing path to the grave and the abject horror of watching it unfold in those we love most dearly.

Because doctors are well-acquainted with the problem, many refuse treatments as their own deaths become imminent. Their goal is to spare themselves and their families the undignified horror and unnecessary expense. Doctors increasingly choose quality over quantity of life when death is imminent.

Dr. Ken Murray has written a great deal on how doctors die, and how it is different from how the rest of us do. Writing for *Reader's Digest*, he describes a case with particulars that are becoming increasingly common:

> Years ago, Charlie, a highly respected orthopedist and a mentor of mine, found a lump in his stomach. The diagnosis was pancreatic cancer. His surgeon was one of the best: He had even invented a new procedure for this exact cancer that could triple the five-year-survival odds—from 5 percent to 15 percent—albeit with a poor quality of life.
>
> Charlie was uninterested. He focused on spending time with family. He got no chemotherapy, radiation, or surgical treatment. Medicare didn't spend much on him. Several months later, he died at home.
>
> Doctors die, of course—but not like the rest of us. What's unusual is not how much treatment they get compared with

most Americans but how little. They have seen what is going to happen, and they generally have access to any medical care they could want. But doctors prefer to go gently.

Most of us approach death only as the doctors' subjects, and we join them in clinging to the last shreds of our own lives. In *The Death of Ivan Ilyich*, Tolstoy laid the delusion bare, writing, "What tormented Ivan Ilyich most was the deception, the lie, which for some reason they all accepted, that he was not dying but was simply ill, and he only need keep quiet and undergo a treatment and then something very good would result."

Medical science cannot grant us immortality, for even if it could extend our natural lifespans indefinitely, accidents, injuries, and eventual global catastrophes will claim our lives. There is certainly nothing wrong with the attempt to live a longer, healthier life so long as the effort continues to recognize two things: more life does not necessarily mean more living, and there is humanity in dying gently. Dying with humanity requires letting go of any hope of living forever.

Deceiving ourselves about our impending mortality by telling tales of eternal life makes for one of our favorite immortality themes, but the overwhelming evidence of life is that we all die. All of us. There's no escaping it, so some cling to a different hope—that there's a way back from death. The second common theme of human immortality stories is *resurrection*.

We cannot even mention the word resurrection without immediately also thinking of religion. The Christian story *is* that Jesus died and was resurrected, and so too shall we be, if we're devout enough. Other religions like Hinduism and Buddhism rely on the same idea but call it *reincarnation*. The connection to morality in these religious immortality stories is explicit. The message is that there is a way to live again after death, and it is achieved by making a certain set of moral attitudes and sincere beliefs core to your life.

Morally charged immortality stories do something more than just deny death; they imbue life with a sense of purpose. "Live rightly so that you too might be resurrected." "All this life is a test to prepare yourself for the next." These are speculations that lend a powerful sense of purpose to human lives. Purpose is a core psychological need, and because it is directly concerned with having spent our time correctly, our notions of meaning in life are often understood morally, in terms of right and wrong living.

Christianity, Judaism, and Islam speculate that sin—deviation from religious moral law—is the reason we die, and so their resurrection beliefs are concerned about sinfulness. Hinduism does much of the same with its notion of *karma*, which is the price for deviating from one's *dharma*, or intended role in life. Because these beliefs concern eternity (often in decadent comfort or hellish torment), they can also completely distort ethical intuitions of those who cling to them to deny death. This we see in religious zealotry that puts more value on devotion to God than on human life and connection, and it is one of the great shames of religion that shows its ugly face far too often. Forever is an incommensurate reward or punishment for any amount of right or wrong living, but it is also the only way to imagine that we have defeated death, which will come later or sooner unless eternity is assured.

The theme of resurrection—sometimes combined with the quest for physical immortality—appears outside of religion, too. When we envision the possibility of advanced future technologies that can put humans into suspended animation, to be revived later, we are appealing to the resurrection theme. Incubator ships to perpetuate humanity on distant worlds constitute a kind of global example. If the purpose of such a pause on the continuity of life is to await a future in which technology has advanced enough to cure us of our diseases or reverse our accumulated aging, then the resurrection theme is little more than a plot vehicle for a broader eternal-life immortality story.

The idea of preserving ourselves for later resurrection is not so alien as it sounds. More familiar variations on the theme are common and can be bizarre and macabre. Sepulchers and other elaborate tombs, along with mummification and embalming of bodies, attend to beliefs that the dead must be prepared for the next life into which they will arise. Whatever the belief system in play, this behavior must speak to a resurrection immortality theme, for if the next life were purely spiritual, there would be no need to preserve the physical body to live in it. In addition to giving rise to some of our most enduring characters of horror— zombies, mummies, and even vampires—beliefs such as these aren't taken lightly. In fact, only a few of our projects can rival them in effort and expense. Consider, for example, the Great Pyramids and the immense labor and suffering that went into their constructions. And to what end?

J. R. R. Tolkien's fiction, which we can turn to again, accounts for the threat hidden in this theme of human vanity. In *The Return of the King*, the third part of his most famous work, *The Lord of the Rings*, Tolkien wrote,

> The old wisdom that was borne out of the West was forsaken. Kings made tombs more splendid than the houses of the living and counted the names of their descent dearer than the names of their sons. Childless lords sat in aged halls musing on heraldry or in high, cold towers asking questions of the stars. And so the people of Gondor fell into ruin.

Tolkien, of course, was writing of a fictional universe, but he spoke deeply to human psychology. Denying our so-called Gift, death, can become an obsession that we take upon ourselves, often to tragic ends.

Our tombs are only sometimes concerned with dreams of resurrection back into the world, though. Many of humanity's elaborate preparations of the dead have been intended to prepare the deceased for an afterlife separate from this world. That is, many of our religious beliefs are less focused upon resurrection than upon *transcendence* of death.

Christianity and Islam often accept transcendent death-denial stories, despite their simultaneous beliefs in resurrection of some kinds. In these religions, transcendence is captured in the idea of Heaven or Paradise when it is believed to be somehow separated from the material world. These religions teach that your spiritual part, believed to be your true part, can go to Heaven when the physical body dies, if you have lived a properly religious life.

Transcendence beliefs go further than the other resurrection themes in their denial of death. Instead of denying the inevitability or permanence of death, transcendence stories deny that death means anything more than the final divorce of the eternal soul from the mortal body. They turn death into a story of long-awaited and often well-earned freedom and reward for a life rightly lived.

Though the beliefs are different, the stories are similar in Hinduism and Buddhism. When you die, these religions teach that the soul detaches from the body so it can reincarnate into another. These religions possess the idea of Heaven as well, treating a lifetime merely as a single step in a far longer moral journey. Hindus and Buddhists believe that ultimately, with enough attendance to religious duties and having learned enough moral lessons, the soul can depart for a paradise entirely removed from the suffering contained in the death-rebirth cycle of life. The immortality projects built out of stories of transcendence lead us to work toward moral perfection so that death is rendered a mere illusion of the world, but they can also lead us to demand perfection of others on our terms.

Themes of transcendence are written in technological language as well. The desire to upload our consciousness into a computer is yet another way to express this same story in a different way. Whether with promises of Heaven or by being uploaded into a computer-generated simulated universe, the transcendence theme says, "Your physical body may die, but the part of you that is really 'you' can live on. Your mind, your consciousness, your 'true self' can be lifted, *deus ex machina*, out of the confines of death and delivered into an undying realm." The hope that technology can be our salvation from death is one aspect of *transhumanism*, the belief that humanity can use science and technology to surpass its present limitations, including mortality. For all its techno-*chic*, the appeal of a transhumanist upload is still just another futile denial of death.

The uploading of human consciousness onto a machine presents a large number of obvious barriers—at this time we have no idea how, or if, it can be accomplished. There is a deeper issue as well. Whatever gets loaded into a machine might be a replica of my consciousness, but it's difficult to make any case that it is *my* consciousness, especially if I am still alive. The moment it gets uploaded, it would also become different and separate, and while it may "live" on after my death, it doesn't do anything to deal with the fact that *I still die*.

There are possible ways in which we could pretend to avoid

the issue that a simulated copy of our consciousness isn't identical to it. Perhaps, for instance, we could upload a consciousness at death. An anesthetized dying person's mind, along with his sense of conscious experience, could be loaded into server in such a way that, from his perspective, his experience changes from the real experience to the simulated one rather in the same way as waking up from a surgery. Whether or not this constitutes continuing to live is a question that's as strange as it is currently pointless.

Further, such circumstances are easily imagined only because they are idealized. Reality is far grimmer for its relentless indifference to our schemes. Deaths are not always predictable, and to be worth doing the uploading of a consciousness surely would have to be done before the final deterioration toward death begins. That means the surest way to upload a mind without it being a mere copy would be to *cause* the biological death of an otherwise healthy individual when the upload is completed. There is almost no ethical case that could be taken seriously for making such a decision, or deciding at which stage in life it should be done.

Even so, uploading ourselves digitally doesn't escape death. *Nothing* does. The server running the simulation, supposing even that it could maintain itself and otherwise avoid failure, needs energy, and there are no unending sources of energy in the universe. Even our machines, ultimately, are mortal. Death, in the sense of a final termination of consciousness, comes eventually, whether it comes at the end of an experience of dying or not. We will die, and if we get our minds onto computer-driven servers and manage to digitally transcend death, those servers eventually die too, taking "us" with them. There is no escaping death, even if technology can potentially offer a solution to prolonging a high-quality living experience for extremely long periods of time.

Clearly, we do not like being reminded that we will die and will go to great lengths to avoid it. We're so exquisitely sensitive to reminders of our mortality, it seems, that we often react to them (with deep currents of denial) even when it seems absurd to do so. These denials of mortality appear to be very deeply wired and operative on the moral level, dictating our reactions before we have a chance to think about them, and still tending to override our thoughts when we do. It requires shockingly little, it seems, to trigger our innate uneasiness with mortality—so little that we eagerly engage in denying the most obvious fact about human beings: that we are animals.

When we are reminded that we are animals, we are reminded that we have brutish impulses we'd rather ignore and, more pressingly, that we are *mortal*. The privacy we seek when going to the bathroom and the perceived obscenity of pornography, which graphically depicts sexual acts, are two examples of how we hide from our mortality by separating ourselves from our animal impulses (and notice the strong moral overtones regarding these topics). Fascinatingly, witnessing breastfeeding also induces this effect by raising the degree to which women objectify other women and themselves. The immortality story at play insists that our humanity is somehow separate from the fact that we are mammals. We'd rather that we are something higher, minds that might not have to die.

Our death-denying sense of transcendence extends deeply into our psychology, giving rise to a principled denial of human nature. The theme runs that our true selves are immaterial and separate from our bodies, and so a significant aspect of the transcendence immortality theme results in treating the human mind like a "blank slate" upon which anything can be written.

Believing our minds to be like blank slates, as though our genetics play no part, has proven as durable as it is unlikely to be true—it has informed many of our models of education and parenting for more than a century.

In addition to feeding our more optimistic fantasies about human society, for example, that people and cultures can be molded like clay merely by teaching them the right values, the blank slate mentality allows us to pretend that we aren't what we are, animals. Animals live lives enslaved to instinct and then die, whereas human beings think, dream, imagine, inspire, create, and love—or so it is commonly felt. Immense cultural architectures have been built to maintain our separateness from animals, from religious beliefs about our role as their masters (a status granted to us, no less, by alleged origins in a special act of creation) to early scientific beliefs that ordered animals "higher" and "lower," with humans higher than the entire taxonomic hierarchy (but lower than saints, angels, and God). Why?

The blank slate mentality typically sees human beings as *mind first and body second*, with attendance to the fact that we're animals almost not at all. We *have* bodies, and we see ourselves as minds. Our physical bodies may die, but for our immaterial minds, who knows? Or so the hope goes. The thought that we are minds ahead of anything else may arise because it feels like we are minds. It also separates us from death, so we want it to be true. This is the heart of the immortality theme of transcendence. But it isn't true. When we die, our minds end. What we each call "I" is an abstract thing, a set of ideas that ends with our deaths. When we die, the term "I" loses its reference. "I" is a philosophical thing that only has meaning so long as we live.

These three themes—physical immortality, resurrection,

and transcendence—give rise to immortality projects possessed by an unfortunate tendency to deny facts or to take up inhumane moralizing. Destructive themes in education, child-rearing, and social engineering, for example, have followed from psychological and social theorizing that denies human nature. Religiously motivated denial of biological evolution, rejections of people (sometimes including one's own children) over matters of birth or belief, and impediments against certain kinds of medical research using embryonic stem cells are specific ways in which these immortality themes have played out to human detriment. All of those beliefs are centered directly upon a Pollyannaish hope that we will not die if we believe the right things.

The soberest, or perhaps the most mature, immortality projects we embrace have a theme of a different fiber: legacy, the mark we will leave on the world. We have a variety of different kinds of legacies available to us, including our genetic legacy in our descendants and the legacies of our work and character. In each case, the immortality story we tell ourselves about our legacies is that even if we do not live beyond our deaths, some part of us will, either in our descendants, in memories, or in the effects we have had upon society.

Compared with the other immortality themes, legacy is easily the least delusional. Where the other themes seek to deny the reality of death, legacy recognizes it, yet attempts to render it less important, even drawing motivation to succeed from the fact of death. Being concerned with our legacies often spurs us to make meaningful impacts that we perhaps would not have made otherwise, but it too comes at a cost.

The immortality story of legacy urges us to seek greatness, and a life in thrall to legacy is an interminable pressure to live a life of legend. But for whom? And for what? And at what cost? Among those rare names we remember from history are many personalities who we remember only in infamy because of their fixations on legacy that led to utter destruction.

Even in the realm of the mundane everyperson, the questions about seeking a life of legend remain cutting. For whom? And for what? And at what cost? For all the value a view to legacy can bring to our work, it is an invitation to miss the locality of most of our lives—and thus of much of what value our lives hold. One of the great regrets people often face near the end of their lives is spending too much time on the wrong kinds of things, including building a legacy when the effort caused them to miss what was nearer to hand and thus far more important. In the end, there is little but love, connection, and the remembered echoes of happiness, and few of us, in our last calculation, will want to be remembered by strangers for greatness so much as we will wish to have been great for those we were closest to, including ourselves.

Whether these four themes—physical immortality, resurrection, transcendence, and legacy—constitute all of the types of stories we tell ourselves to deny death does not matter. The reality of death and eventual extinction proves each, in whatever language or time it is written, to be a human vanity. Our usual response to the resulting existential dread is to cling even more tightly to our immortality projects as a way of distracting ourselves from our ultimate despair: not just death, but meaninglessness.

The author of Ecclesiastes only had it *almost* right. It's not that *everything* is vanity; it's that our immortality projects are. Immortality stories and the projects built upon them steal our innate understanding of the purposes that mean the most in our lives. Death is necessarily close at hand and far more mundane than our fear and arrogance might have us wish. In the end, we'll regret not having lived in every moment that we wasted hoping never to die. These are regrets, however, that can be avoided.

RELIGION AND DEATH

*For God so loved the world that he gave his one
and only Son, that whoever believes in him shall
not perish but have eternal life.*

—John 3:16, NIV

We cannot continue from our discussion of the denial of death without putting considerable attention on the broadest and most vigorous of humanity's immortality projects: religion.

If Ernest Becker was right about using moral projects to effect a denial of death, it follows from religion's preoccupation with death that religion would make moralizing its central occupation. The primary purpose for the majority of religions in the world may be denying the reality of death, and moral instruction is certainly their next most obvious endeavor. Religious immortality stories deny the reality of death by insisting on the reality of the soul, and the fate and quality of the soul are understood religiously in almost explicitly moral terms.

For those who believe in it, religious or not, the soul is seen as the most essential part of a human being. Most religions tell the story that if we are good, an expressly moral concept, our souls are promised either rebirth or the pleasures of Heaven. Should we be bad and unrepentant for our sin, however, we are told that we will face either a cursed next life, annihilation of the immortal part of ourselves, or final damnation by banishment to an infernal eternity of punishment—fates we usually reserve for our impenitent moral enemies and yet dread for ourselves. In service to these beliefs, the world's religions tell some of our most elaborate immortality stories.

The central promise of most religions is that death is either not real or not final, but that salvation from death is not guaranteed. Most religions insist we must prove ourselves worthy of invitation, and the story goes that death might be avoided by right living. This structure makes religions intrinsically concerned with morality. Morality is so central to religions that the most general characterization of religions begins by identifying them as a kind of *moral community*.

It is fitting here to point out that I'm referring to morals in a way that not everyone does. I separate *human values* and *morals* into two distinct categories. I use "morality" to refer to a cultural feature that attempts to approximate human values. This is why different cultures and, especially, different religions have such different morals, and it's why sentences like "their morals are immoral" are perfectly clear to us in their meaning.

Religions act as moral communities for two reasons: death and life. Living in communities requires morality to make them functional, and religions are broad-reaching frameworks that aim to keep their flocks on largely the same moral pages. Many of the effects of religious communities are highly beneficial. They bring their communities together, increase trust, promote moral behavior, and provide a contextual narrative that fosters believers' senses of personal and community identity. Thus religions manage life.

Because of their centrality in life for adherents, the social benefits of religion come with certain costs. Like all moral communities equipped with beliefs deemed sacred—that is, beyond question—religion's social advantages tend to be parochial. Religions increase trust and community cohesion mostly within the faith and sometimes not at all outside of it, and lines are often drawn explicitly in moral terms. A common problem with morally charged groups is that, for all the improvements in social behaviors they cause within the group, they can also lead to hostility toward those outside of it. This issue leaves religions and other moral tribes particularly vulnerable to sectarian distrust, disagreement, and even violence. Because religious beliefs help people manage their terror of death and offer a promise of immortality, these problems sometimes generate extremism—the terror of death is sometimes managed by murdering those who threaten a religious's immortality narrative.

Religions help people manage death in that they attempt to explain it while placing it in a broader context: the faith's prevailing moral, cultural, and immortality narratives. For the righteous, there is the assurance of Heaven, favorable reincarnation, or escape from the cycles of worldly suffering. Upon the evil, justice will be served. In this way, the cultural narratives provided by religion are immortality stories, and the rites, duties, and moral requirements of the faith are their immortality projects.

The specific stories by which religion denies death are worth considering in more detail. Heaven promises comfort, richness, communion, and (perhaps not as often) decadence and pleasure. (Doesn't this tell us more about what we wish for in life than what we fear in death?) It is a fate far better than dying, but only for those deemed worthy.

Hell is the opposite, promising torture and separation to an eternal outcast. Its more lurid descriptions seem to speak volumes to the potency of the sadism accessible to human imagination. These include physical pain, backbreaking and pointless labor, humiliation, festering disease, unendurable torment, and utter isolation. These are easily understood to be fates against which death can easily be construed as a mercy, proving that oblivion is, indeed, the "Gift of Men"—at least compared to sufficient suffering. They, too, tell us more about what we want to avoid in life than what we fear in death.

Hell, it bears noting, is also a fate *reserved for others*—fewer than 2 percent of people who believe Hell exists believe that they, themselves, might go there. This chilling statistic tells us something about how badly we can regard our moral enemies and how easily we can dehumanize them and their potential for suffering. Even those who do not believe in Hell can be caught wishing there were such a place for people they deem bad enough. Reflection upon such dark facets of human nature should urge us to take the human need for justice seriously and to be better people while we do it. Our impulses to coarse retribution should rarely feel more ignoble than when we wish an inescapable eternity of hellfire on someone.

In some traditions, as with most of Christianity and Islam, Heaven and Hell are concepts with *infinite* value or cost, if only by virtue of their eternity. The problem with such beliefs is that any attempt to make sense of the rewards and costs within a justice system is completely ruined by injecting an infinite value or cost.

To understand how, we need some appreciation of the immeasurable scale of infinity. The easiest way to get it (recognizing that not everyone loves abstract mathematics) is to start with the biggest number you can think of. Pick one. It doesn't matter what number you picked; that number is smaller than most numbers. Maybe you chose some "big" number like a trillion, which has a mere thirteen digits. It doesn't matter. Against infinity, any number you might have picked is so tiny that essentially *every* number is bigger.

That's a counterintuitive statement, but the logic is fairly accessible. If you chose a trillion, there are a trillion numbers between one and the number you chose. To be sure, that's a lot of numbers, but it's only a trillion of them. A trillion can be doubled to get two trillion, and that can be doubled to get four trillion. And when would this have to stop? Never. Unbelievable as it may seem, mathematicians have demonstrated that the set of numbers larger than a trillion has *exactly the same* cardinality (which measures quantity, to speak roughly) as *all* of the numbers. A trillion, even a trillion trillions or a trillion-digit number, is no "closer to" infinity than one is.

Perhaps it doesn't make sense to quantify justice, however intuitive it may seem, but against a promise of infinite reward or a threat of infinite punishment, literally any value applied to the finite transgressions of our finite lives is effectively meaningless. That means that any behavior, no matter how heinous, that is done in expectation of receiving an infinite reward or avoiding an infinite cost can be rationalized once the set of scales is broken by placing an infinity on one side. Religious immortality stories containing promises of infinite rewards and costs—like Heaven and Hell—are therefore some of humanity's most reliable engines for generating disproportionate (read: bad) moral judgments and thus unnecessary human misery.

Religious immortality narratives aren't all Heaven and Hell. Another is the doctrine of reincarnation. It suggests that after we die, the immortal soul-like essence it assumes does not die but is reborn into another life. According to some traditions, a person may be reborn higher or lower in the grand hierarchy of being, and each lifetime can therefore be understood as little more than a lesson in right-living. Learn the lessons, and you reboot next time with a better life. Maybe you'll be richer, have more status, be famous, or be luckier. Fail to learn your lessons or reject them, and you'll come back in even worse shape—poorer, less healthy, unluckier, or not even human. Belief in reincarnation may superficially seem just, but it's yet another powerful engine of human misery.

The notion of reincarnation is actually stunning in its capacity to justify, and thus quietly accept, horrific injustices. Every physical, social, and economic disadvantage or injustice that human beings have ever cruelly visited upon one another—with slavery well within the ranks—can be interpreted through the lens of doctrines of reincarnation to be something that was *deserved* merely for the accidents of one's birth. There is nothing for you to do but bear the burden of your suffering and know that you deserve it, hoping to extract the right lessons so that you might not have it so bad the next time around. Ironically, some people call this "hopeful."

The opposite side of this perspective is worse. Reincarnation also suggests that power, prestige, wealth, undue advantage, and every other conceivable good fortune in life are *earned* by doing nothing more than being born as you were. Reincarnation insists that the true you, in a past lifetime you cannot hope to remember, earned your good luck for you and thus entitled you to it. Where it comes to entrenching worldly miseries arising from social injustices, the detached whim of Heaven has nothing on the doctrine of reincarnation.

Take a moment to notice that all of these denials of death are, by any account, wildly popular. More people believe in religious immortality stories than any other kind. One reason, of course, is that they provide a direct route to avoiding the terror of death and existential dread. There are other reasons for their popularity too, and they are probably more important.

The denial of death is typically achieved by the quest for purpose in life. All reward-based immortality projects share a sense that life has an overarching purpose, and in particular life's inequities and suffering aren't in vain. If you make it to Heaven, then all your misfortunes will be recompensed in Paradise. If you reincarnate, the point of your misery is the lessons that you learn from it. In both cases, your rewards will have been earned, and thus the worst trials of your life will have positive *meaning*. Ensconced in the denial of death is giving meaning both to life and the suffering contained within it, and this is the central message of every religion on the planet.

Religion, however, has no monopoly on human psychology, including the human drive to deny death. It does, perhaps, attend to our fear of death with more enthusiasm and acceptance than any other human endeavor, but all of our immortality projects are expressions of the same needs. Those needs are, primarily, to feel meaning in our lives and to avoid the immense psychological discomfort of gazing upon death honestly.

The denial of death, however, proves a true and enduring

obstacle to living fully. Death is hard enough to face as it is, and immortality stories make it far more difficult. It's hardly possible to understand the implications that death must have on life without accepting its full reality, and what barrier to the acceptance of death could be more complete than its outright denial?

For myself, I do not think I could have seen life in light of death had it not been the case that I lost my faith first. My faith was too hopeful an insulator from the bare fact of death. In this case, though, honestly facing the truth is difficult even without faith. It took several years after I stopped believing in God and Heaven for the inescapable and obvious truth that *I have this life, and that's all I get* to sink in and start to influence my thoughts. It took longer still for me to be able to come face-to-face with the fact.

To see our own lives clearly, we first have to overcome the denial of death. There is no other way. To overcome the denial of death requires facing death head-on and accepting it, and that requires overcoming our deep-seated fears of death itself and of dying.

THE FEAR OF DEATH

Death is nothing to us, since when we are,
death has not come,
and when death has come, we are not.

—Epicurus

Where do we go when we die?

"We" don't go anywhere when we die. Upon death, that which makes up the *"we"* in the question loses its concrete meaning. Becoming less than the meanest ghost when we die, "we" become nothing more than recollections, stories, and legacy, insubstantial and temporary things to be enjoyed for a while and slowly forgotten over not more than a few generations. Horrible as this sounds, embracing these facts can take away most of our fear of death.

Our fears of death and dying are instinctual, as close as reflexes, and deeply unpleasant to contemplate. These fears are also exaggerated, and the reflexive discomfort we feel about the terror of death is often what prevents us from seeing the matter clearly.

Viewed impassively the fears surrounding our own deaths make little sense, and when we think about how our loved ones would want us to take their deaths, it is the same. It isn't even that we should think death won't be bad; it's that "bad" isn't a qualifier applicable to being dead. In fact, *no qualifier* applies to "being dead," which itself is a phrase that speaks more to our terror than to sense. When we talk about "being dead," we are lying to ourselves, misleading ourselves by our very language to believe that there is some experience of death. This tendency is little more than an unavoidable confusion among the living, for whom death is incomprehensible. That which we mean by "I" is never dead.

This particular confusion runs deep and is only partly just semantic. Some of what we mean by "I" is the imagined continuity over a lifetime of the person identifying herself that way, a sense that extends into the realm of memory once she has died. In that way, a statement like "she is dead" seems to make sense, but it doesn't quite work. She died. The personality that was "she" doesn't exist after she has died, and only temporary memories remain. "She is dead" is a linguistic and conceptual shortcut that belies a deep-running human lack of willingness to confront the finality of death honestly. Take a moment to appreciate the difference in how the two sentences feel, in fact, even though they convey the same information: "she is dead" versus "she died." The first expresses an idea connected to finality in some present tense after the end, and the second directly indicates finality through the past tense. The second sentence feels colder and harder to bear as a result. In thinking about death, it can be very, very hard to do without being tempted to insert being where being isn't.

Analogies are tempting but unhelpful for making sense of what it is like to be dead because it isn't like anything to be dead. Being dead is the precise opposite of being, at all. A very popular comparison (among those who do not believe in an afterlife) is that "being dead" is qualitatively the same as what it is like before being born. This is true enough in a vacuous way, but it confers absolutely no substance or clarity. In fact, for all the thought it may jog, it relies upon precisely the same error as lies at the heart of the phrase "being dead." "We" weren't before we were born either, so the analogy just compares the unfathomable to the unimaginable.

We more commonly connect death and sleep. "Rest in peace," we say, and sometimes we call death the "Big Sleep." Likening death to sleep is nothing more than an admission that we lack conscious awareness after we die, but the comparison is bad and seduces us with false comfort because it denies death.

Sleep is something the living do, and it isn't even something that is fully unconscious. Not only do we dream while we sleep—and often remember our dreams—but we also wake, both in the middle of the night and when we have slept long enough. Sleep can only be likened to death in that for some portions of it we lay still, are oblivious to the world outside our minds, and, in its deepest phases, register no conscious awareness. During truly unconscious sleep, however, we have absolutely no experiences, retain no memories, and simply miss time. Deep sleep, then, is a temporary pause of consciousness, appreciated for its restfulness but not missed, while death is its permanent termination, beyond which appreciation, rest, wanting, and time have no subjective meaning.

A more potent "experience" of unconsciousness is available medically with general anesthesia, but even this offers us no insight into the nature of death. To be "put under" is at once surreal and utterly vacant. In one moment you get overwhelmingly drowsy, and in the next you awake groggy and disoriented only to find out with some surprise that the procedure is over (or, as in my case once, that the oral surgeon is breaking your wisdom teeth with some maniacal tool and you cannot tell him you are awake because your mouth is clamped fully open). People have elaborate surgeries and even sometimes temporarily die (by the clinical definition) while under general anesthesia, and until consciousness returns after the fact, they are none the wiser. The attempt to draw an analogy between death and being generally anesthetized illuminates nothing. It merely points unhelpfully to the only part of a significant ordeal that, though it is lived through, isn't *experienced* at all. The price of the comparison is inviting the death-denying error at the heart of the resurrection theme: that one's own death can somehow be described simultaneously in the first person and in the past tense.

Death is not like sleep, and it is only "like" anesthesia if something goes badly enough so that you don't wake up (and thus actually die, killing the analogy). Death is the beginning of the total, irrevocable, and permanent absence of experience. In one moment, things are happening, whether they are pleasant or not, and then, in the next—. And there is no waking up. All there is, is—, and in terms of experienced moments, there isn't even—.

So, we tend to see death falsely, imagining it as though through the eyes of an unreal contradiction, a dead conscious experience, but this is an illusion generated by a mind that literally cannot escape itself. Death is thoroughly unintelligible because oblivion defies contemplation (although it may really be that contemplation defies oblivion). For all of the ranging freedom of human imagination, it is permanently and inexorably constrained by the quality of being aware. Even if we live through consciousness-canceling ordeals like general anesthesia, conscious experience doesn't go along for the ride—and that's quite the point. It is, of course, possible to imagine the world without us in it, but to imagine being dead is impossible because death isn't a state of being.

This point of view isn't original. It isn't even remotely new. The Greek philosopher Epicurus recognized more than two thousand years ago that death is not a part of life. The Austrian philosopher Ludwig Wittgenstein realized the same a little over a century ago. These philosophers understood the most important fact about death: we do not experience it and thus have no reason to fear death in itself.

A more recent thinker, the eloquent commentator Christopher Hitchens, pondering Death's unsparing invitation (written in the form of advanced esophageal cancer), put to phrase part of what Epicurus and Wittgenstein avoided. He worded it metaphorically, remarking that the existential issue at the heart of death that bothered him most isn't so much that the party is ending but rather that it is most assuredly going on—though without you in it.

For all its poignancy, this party metaphor is not about the dead. It is the kind of thought that can only impact the living. It should therefore help us, who yet exist, illuminate how we should live, knowing Death's note will come to us someday as well and cannot be refused.

In the metaphor, denying death is pretending either that we

never have to leave the party at all, or that we only step out so we can attend another (hopefully better) one somewhere else. These are tragic views that threaten to diminish the party we already attend. They invite us to take what we have for granted, wherein we exchange the moments of our lives for the mere passage of time.

Denying death isn't merely believing the best is yet to come; it is misaligning our priorities around the notion that the best can only arrive after all we have now has ended. Such a belief turns our one chance to live into an audition in which the great hope in our performance is securing invitations to some bigger show for ourselves and our loved ones. However crass it may seem to say so, it must be added as well that literally no one can truly know there is any bigger show to get into—and that there are good reasons to accept that there's not even the consolation of a smaller one. These displacements can and do cause good people to while away their lives and to frustrate their relationships, which in the end are all that they will have ever had.

Even without denial, when we envision death as leaving the great party of life, we tend to do it forgetting the utter incomprehensibility of oblivion. The mind, once detached from the terror of death, tends to find this point easily, but it is very hard to maintain the thought. Sadness and dread creep back in with the inevitable realization that *we* are the party-goers, and our part in the party means *our very lives*. The party, our attendance, and our ultimate departure from it are therefore perfectly personal.

If you imagine the scene following your last goodbyes in the imagery of leaving a party, it might tend to start with how you'll make your exit. If you are lucky, you'll realize it's time to go with time enough to make your goodbyes in your own way before

LIFE IN LIGHT OF DEATH ☠ 69
an easy, graceful glide to and out of the door. Maybe your exit will be showy and tearful, and maybe you'll quietly slip away. If you're less lucky, you'll be ushered out quickly or, taking a wrong turn, open the front door by mistake, perhaps looking for your coat or another bottle of wine, and step accidentally into your own oblivion.

We often imagine those dearest to us will be there waiting just outside the door, and our most hopeful immortality stories tell us they will be. It may be so, but we have no reasons beyond imagination and hope to think so. More certain is that we will want them there as we make our way down the hall. In the end, our relationships and the love they have been filled with will be most of what matters, and that tells us much about how we should spend our time. We must nourish our relationships while we can.

The hard truth, however, is that when it's time to go, in every case, we all take the last step utterly alone.

That we leave isn't the hard part, nor is that we all leave alone. If we think about it, even that the party will be going on without us isn't so bad. At least it's going on, for a little while, anyway. The really tough part of death is watching other people leave, never to return, and knowing that as they go, they take some of our festivity with them. This is what makes understanding that the party continues in our absence hit us the hardest—not what, but who, remains, and what our departures will mean to them. The only thing for it, then, is to make the most of our time while we have the chance. We live for those who live through our "party" with us, just as they live for us in return, and when even the least of us leaves, those who stay and remember will grieve. Yet, they can also find joy in the very fact that we were ever there.

When at last we come to our own departures, we may

imagine ourselves stepping out into the night, climbing down the front stairs, and strolling down a dim sidewalk toward … somewhere—maybe someplace where we can think back on what we did and about what we might be missing out on now that we've gone. We are wrong to do so.

There will not be any looking back once you go. There will be no sitting and thinking, no stroll down the sidewalk, and no climb down the front stairs. The reality of death is that in the very instant you leave, just as you step out, even before the door closes at last behind you, from your perspective there isn't even *nothing*, and the mind you consider *you* no longer is.

Saying there is nothing after death demands elaboration, but no elaboration is possible. The nothingness of death is the kind of nothing that simply isn't. To attempt to describe it would fail because merely attempting to imagine it makes it into something—and something it isn't. From your perspective, once you leave the party, there is no party. There isn't even the memory of one because your perspective ends when you go. Looking back only happens before you leave, and whether you have something worth looking back upon will impact your enjoyment of your latest moments.

Even contemplating what it means to miss out on that part of the party that continues after we have to leave is something we only do while we are alive. Those thoughts, then, are *part of the party*. Lingering remorse over the fact that we will one day certainly leave may sometimes shade the mood, but it cannot change that we have just one chance to celebrate.

That you'll be going at the height of festivities hardly matters. Of course you will! It is *always* the height of festivities, even if we misplace the ability to realize it. Life is just one of those kinds of parties, and to understand the point is to rob

Death of his terror. The question, then, isn't about where we go when we die; it's about where we can take ourselves while we live.

Facing death is a worthwhile part of life, but brooding upon it is not. To worry about it is pointless, and to spend our lives ruminating is to miss the best of living. From each of our own perspectives, *our time at the party is literally all that there ever is*, and such a gift shouldn't be wasted. We only need to live fully enough to have something worth reflecting happily upon in the company of those we treasure if we wish to make the most of our lives. To live in light of death is to make the most of the time we each have left in which to connect and to enjoy ourselves.

DYING

This is what has made it so simple to shoot down whole herds of buffalo or elephants. The animals don't know that death is happening and continue grazing placidly while others drop alongside them. The knowledge of death is reflective and conceptual, and animals are spared it. They live and they disappear with the same thoughtlessness: a few minutes of fear, a few seconds of anguish, and it is over. But to live a whole lifetime with the fate of death haunting one's dreams and even the most sun-filled days—that's something else.

—*Ernest Becker, in* The Denial of Death

But then, there's dying.

Dying is a process within life, the last endurance of the living, and it is scary. It is how we make our way to the door, and our exits can be smooth, graceful, and even cheerful, but

73

they may not be. Although life sometimes slips away gently, living things often do not die easily, and it isn't by accident that much of what can kill us does so painfully. Our fear of dying, then, is primarily composed of a fear of dying *badly*. We can rest assured, however, that this, too, is a fear we both misplace and exaggerate.

Dying has no parallel in life because there is no continuation after death. Like every event we experience, our exit from life will be a temporary affair, one that lasts a little while and then is over. Unlike anything else in life, when dying is over, it is truly over. Because our memories will be among the casualties of our deaths, we will not remember any suffering that kills us. This seemingly obvious point turns out to be important.

Any suffering in dying is truly temporary, which puts it completely outside of our reference. With any pain that does not kill us, we have to contend with the fact that we will remember much of our suffering and will be changed by the experience— and that we anticipate the stress of both the memory and the change. This is not applicable in death. Death brings not relief but a final end. The difference is not subtle if we know *how* we remember past experiences and prepare for future ones, particularly ones in which we suffer.

We are predisposed to remember according to a rule of thumb known as the peak-end rule. This psychological heuristic suggests the most intense and the last moments of an experience frequently have the greatest impact upon how we will recollect it. Suppose, for instance, we undergo some uncomfortable minor medical procedure under local anesthesia. If the medical professionals have done their jobs well, the peak experience will be the moment of the injection of the anesthetic (and not staring up in helpless horror at an operating oral surgeon). We usually remember peak experiences and use them to inform our decisions.

The more interesting part of the peak-end rule is the influence that the end of an experience has on how we remember it. When experiences end well, we tend to remember them more positively than when they don't, and our behavior reflects this quirk about the processes of memory.

The peak-end rule used to play a significant role in colonoscopies before doctors began to do the exams under general "twilight" anesthesia. Patients were observed to be more likely to return for their next scheduled colonoscopy if the tail end of the uncomfortable procedure was intentionally softened. When colonoscopies were done as quickly as possible to minimize the total discomfort, rates of patient return visits were lower than in cases where doctors apparently needlessly prolonged the end of the examination. The result was that colonoscopies often included leaving the scope in place and doing nothing procedural with it for the last few minutes of the exam. Even though the uncomfortable scope remained inserted longer than necessary, patients in those circumstances were much more likely to return for their next routine checkup than their peers for whom doctors butted out more quickly.

The peak-end effect is believed to be caused by certain biases in how we store and consider memories that relate to how we conceive of ourselves. In some ways, we possess something like two distinct mental selves. One self *experiences*, and the other *remembers*.

The experiencing self is, as the name suggests, the part of us having an experience. It feels pain and pleasure, and it feels them now. The remembering self is a mental construction of ourselves in reflection. It does not feel pain or pleasure. It recalls *that* we felt, along with details describing what we felt. You may have noticed that when you are not sick, you mercifully cannot reproduce the *feeling of* being sick. On the other hand, if you are sick, well—I'm sorry to tell you what you already surely realize; you can't help yourself by conjuring what it feels like to be well. Sensory neurons, it could be said, may be more enlightened than many cortical ones—they live in the now.

The part of you that remembers what it is like to stay up too late and drink too much (which you might call "night you") is the remembering self. It knows what it is doing to the you that will wake up feeling awful tomorrow ("morning you"), but it can't feel it. When you try to make up your mind about staying up a little longer, your remembering self (often called "better sense") goes to war with your experiencing self, for which the morning is irrelevant because it doesn't exist. Wisdom, in at least one regard, is learning to listen to the lessons kept by the remembering self.

When it comes to making good decisions about the future, the remembering self is the one we have to appeal to. The experiencing self is too busy living in this moment, as it immediately arises and withers into the next, to inform decisions of this kind, but the remembering self keeps track of how things went before and can guess at what it will put the experiencing self through next time.

To make the calculation, the remembering self combines memories about the peak and end experiences we had in similar circumstances, and a low-intensity finish is something it truly appreciates. If the remembering self rates a past experience as "not that bad" or better, we're likely to recall it positively unless the peak was really awful, and it usually relies significantly on the peak-end rule to decide if that's the case.

We are intimately familiar with the ways in which the peak-end rule shapes our decision making, even if we have never heard of it. The majority of the experiences we have endured and then used to make decisions utilize the ways in which the peak-end rule shades our memories and our plans. That is, the peak-end rule is a part of our cognitive architecture, and for that reason it is able to fool us about how bad dying will be. The result is an exaggeration of our innate dread of life's last experience.

Most of us consider dying at some point in our lives. In the process, without meaning to, we apply the peak-end rule to it, assessing it as an experience that will probably be bad and then worst on the end. Dying ends in death, after all, which is usually a pretty good predictor of an experience going bad, and it's easy to imagine that the worst moment comes right at the end when we actually die. Our reliance upon the peak-end rule tells us that experiences of that kind are awful in their very essence, and for good reason: most are. That dying marks our very last experience, the end of all endings, makes it into a special case that heightens our concerns.

It isn't only because dying carries the aura of being intrinsically bad that the peak-end rule succeeds in magnifying our fears. The potency of our horror swells upon the threat that dying may be bad and the certainty that it will be *last*. Our assessments of dying can be so effectively persuaded by the peak-end rule that we are often misled to believe that our entire lives will be somehow diminished merely by a bad end.

This misplaced concern, of course, is for ourselves mostly bleak hyperbole. That dying is the last thing we can experience doesn't make it more awful, and that it marks the end makes it less.

What goes wrong is that, when we think about dying,

we tend to look at it through the imagined experiences of an anticipated rememberer who will never exist. We skew our evaluation of our last moments by falling for the illusion that we will persist to remember it. We will not.

Sometimes we cling to beliefs that we will, however. Our immortality stories often tell us so, and so they lure us with false hope into an unnecessary misery. Any beliefs we hold about death being other than what it plainly appears to be—the *end* of life—can strengthen the peak-end rule's misleading influence in assessing dying. Such beliefs carry the assumption that there will be a self that remembers dying—you. Believing in Heaven and reincarnation may soothe our fear of death but *increase* our fear of dying.

Throwing off the illusion that we will remember our death does nothing to diminish our hope for a gentle end to our lives, but it can abate some of our fears of dying. It cannot be overstated that dying necessarily differs from every other experience we will ever have because we will not remember it. We can't pretend that dying is never a terrible experience, because it sometimes is, but it is unlikely to be anything as bad as we anticipate.

We may fear dying less for ourselves than for those who will survive us. They will not want us to suffer, just as we would not want them to, and we don't want to leave them with gruesome memories if we do, indeed, meet a bad end. Most of us would prefer to avoid embarrassing them if possible too—think of the testament to the worth of some reasonable caution in life provided by the ignoble Darwin Awards. Embarrassment aside, understanding the peak-end rule can help assuage the worry. If it is true for ourselves, then it is true for others, and so we are at least as likely to exaggerate the suffering involved in the deaths of our loved ones as we are of our own.

We can do nothing but remember that the dying are still living, even if hope of continuance has gone. In that fact is the reminder of the worth of kindness and connection with them until the last and a chance to remind them, if it is we who are dying, that we hope for little more than the same. Few are the tragedies greater than when, in their fear of death, people forsake their dying loved ones in their final weeks, days, or hours. Those moments present a unique opportunity for healing, connection, grieving, reconciliation, love, and acceptance, and they are, if possible, not to be missed.

A portion of our fear of dying, then, is revealed: a fear of dying *unexpectedly*. This fear is disconnected from the peak-end rule and proves the importance of our connections to others in life. To die unexpectedly is to leave no opportunity for the gifts unique to being able to say goodbye, and in being able to plan to have to do it. This fear should be a reminder that those we love can benefit from our prudence, just as we can benefit from theirs. We cannot eliminate calamity, but we can minimize it by balancing it against the opportunities of living.

Most of the rest of our fear of dying, however, is actually a fear of dying *badly*. Suppose you could know that you are going to die gently in your sleep after some comfortable day in the long-distant future. It is a fair guess that your fear of dying immediately drops dramatically even by considering the possibility. Your fear of death may remain, but it feels nice to believe dying could be a peaceful and easy affair. The influence of the "end" portion of the peak-end rule is the reason.

We can make this point far more strongly by imagining a hypothetical drug with a 100 percent chance of killing anyone who takes it, but not before providing them with an overwhelmingly positive experience. The drug would be designed to induce a kind of bliss that defies even our wildest elysian fantasies, rendering our last experience in life painless, free, expansive, wondrous, orgasmic, euphoric, nirvanic— the Platonic epitome of any other glorious adjective we could utter—and then it would kill you, nice and easy. We might imagine the whole affair to be chemically arranged to ease conscious experience at the last from unimaginable pleasure into the bliss of a sunset of warm comfort and cozy, floating drowsiness, under a bath of calm, slowly dimming golden light. In other words, this drug would provide a perfect guarantee that one's last experience would be of Heaven.

Such a drug isn't too fantastical. It would be little more than a suicidal extension of general anesthesia, except that instead of starting by fading into groggy oblivion, everything would become impossibly perfect, like some blend of psychedelic compounds like dimethyltryptamine (DMT), psilocybin, lysergic acid diethylamide (LSD), and mood-altering amphetamines like methylenedioxymethamphetamine (commonly known as ecstasy). Eventually, the trip to Heaven would end, fading into the usual anesthetized oblivion. Of course, this wouldn't be some Lazarus cocktail: instead of the usual death-and-resurrection cycle of general anesthesia, there would be no waking up. We would take it intending its last effect, and that would be the entire point.

The influence of the peak-end rule on our fears of dying is no doubt already becoming clear—dying doesn't seem nearly as bad if a bad end can be easily avoided—but to sharpen it, now imagine a slight variation to this hypothetical drug. Suppose, instead of guaranteeing a wonderful experience that transitions smoothly into death, the drug sometimes goes wrong. Consider the possibility that in 10 percent of recipients, the drug generates the most unendurable suffering imaginable until at last, without abating, it kills. Rather than taking the dying to Heaven, it would cast some unpredictable few into a perfect hell that need not be described in any detail to make the point.

The idea of this drug, which you may have found yourself quite warm to just moments ago, seems terrifying now, doesn't it? And it would still seem terrifying if it only went disastrously wrong in a very tiny fraction of its recipients, say one in ten thousand. Who would take such a drug against these odds? Would you? At the very least, most who might consider it would have quite the mental wrestling match ahead of the decision if it carried even staggeringly low odds of a hellish misfire.

This is where we find the point, then. Both of these hypothetical drugs end in exactly the same way—death—and yet the merest chance that the drug will go terribly wrong drastically changes our assessment of it. Even on very low statistical odds of it taking us to Hell, the balance tips from it seeming like a blessing to an absolute horror. Put another way, if we knew we had to die by being run over by a slow-moving steamroller, no matter how much more interesting the experience would be for it to take us feet-first, most of us would eagerly choose that it roll over us the other way around. That, more accurately, is the fear of *dying badly*, not the fear of dying, and not the fear of death.

When we see these fears clearly for what they are, we also see how the mistake skews our thoughts on the whole affair of death and dying. Our fear of dying badly pointedly makes us uncomfortable, often anxious, and the feeling can be too strong to examine death calmly. Distinguishing the fear of death and the fear of dying badly can go a long way toward easing some of the anxiety that makes it so difficult to face the topic of death honestly. That is, the fear of dying badly obscures the mirror of death and interferes with the view we might otherwise have of living. When we see it for what it is and set it aside, we have an opportunity to learn a lot about how to live better lives.

Turning our attention back to the kinder form of our imaginary drug that lets us imagine the possibility of dying cheerfully on our own terms, we can learn more than just that we fear dying badly by considering it. Take a moment to imagine it like it were already real. What would happen if such a drug were available, and what lessons can we draw from it?

Among the first thoughts to arise is one as obvious as it is chilling. A moment's contemplation tells us that such a drug would have to be strictly controlled because of the incredible number of foolish and impulsive suicides it would certainly precipitate if it could be easily obtained. One bad enough day would do it for many if it were near to hand. Even more sober-minded people, given the chance, would choose a pleasant end over a bad one and would erroneously conclude too soon that the optimal time has arrived, discounting the subtle joys of advancing age or that the winds of fate sometimes shift to the pleasant—half of the time, in fact, to speak statistically, and more often still, to speak psychologically.

Still, few would fail to appreciate the opportunity to end life comfortably on their own terms, as part of the dread of dying is that it awakens fears of our ultimate powerlessness. Dying need not be terrible or outside of our control, and the idea of a drug that causes an easy, perfect suicide makes these points clear. The clear lessons are that living better lives is a worthwhile goal and the fear of dying badly constitutes most of what we identify as the fear of death.

In admitting people would prefer a gentle way out under their own power, we have arrived at the front door to a heated debate that, for all its immense humanitarian significance, is deeply hindered by our terror of death and beliefs we adopt to deny it. Heaven help us, beliefs about an afterlife present the stiffest resistance against death with dignity (and, slightly more broadly, medically assisted suicide).

It requires nothing more than open eyes to recognize that a human life can become awful enough to justify a merciful end. The fact is so obvious that we have to torture the word "premature" to use it to describe a death in such circumstances. Life can become so bad and reach a state with so little hope of improvement that forcing Death's hand by a medically assisted death with dignity will not feel too soon at all, although it may feel too late. All it takes is considering the potential complications leading up to our own demise to conclude we all know it, too.

As the hypothetical drug illustrates, our fears of death and dying are needlessly increased by denying ourselves the possibility of dying with dignity. If much of our fear of dying, and thus of death, is more accurately captured in the fear of dying badly, death with dignity offers us a simple escape from that grinding dismay. One enormous concern for many people is that they will die only after a long, painful fight with some horrible cancer or debilitating disease. They will not know how long their suffering will continue, only that it will, perhaps in terrible cycles of improvement and degeneration, and that it may be characterized by the worst experiences of their lives. The most sadomasochistic aspect of living under this anxiety is that it is almost entirely unnecessary because we do have the means to afford escapes from it ever being fully realized. We call such an escape "death with dignity."

Death with Dignity

All that stands between us and a better conversation about death with dignity are the terror of death and the immortality projects that service it. Refusing the possibility of death with dignity is the result of our immortality projects, and we can see that fact no more clearly than noticing it is an imposition we place uniquely upon human lives. In our vanity and terror, only *human* lives are deemed worthy of a forced final march through Nature's unflinching reminders—irremediable sickness, pain, and degeneration—that She cannot care about our suffering. A horrible end, then, may be universally agreed to be among the worst possible fates in life, and yet it is one we visit solely upon ourselves—routinely, needlessly, and literally with religious devotion.

The quantity of unnecessary human suffering generated by religious opposition to death with dignity is mind-boggling if considered in earnest. To oppose death with dignity in service to an immortality story is to force ourselves, and worse, other people facing the ends of their lives, to die more slowly and painfully than needed. It is to encourage hopeless medical interventions that genuinely are worse than useless. It is to curse the grieving friends and family of the dying with having to watch their loved ones suffer pitifully, and then to request they pay exorbitantly for the opportunity. It is to let the cruelties of biology tear dying people unnecessarily away from their last possession, their dignity. It is to prevent mercy by unjustly calling it murder. And it is to do all of this primarily to protect certain immortality stories we have written so that we may deny death.

The ethical questions concerning death with dignity therefore do not lie in whether or not it should be available;

even having that debate is already a moral failure. The discussion need only concern how we might reliably determine when the time to end a broken life has come. Nothing in the nature of any of our immortality projects, including faith, adds anything of substance to that already difficult debate. An honest discussion of death with dignity demands acknowledging and accepting death, and such a view favors death with dignity.

Both death with dignity and the idea of a route to a perfect death take us to the unpleasant fact of suicide. It may seem that I have made a case *for* suicide, but I have not, at least not in general. Ethically performed medically assisted suicides like deaths with dignity have to be done under the guidance of qualified medical professionals, including representatives of psychiatric care. Outside of those narrow bounds, suicide is unlikely to be ethically defensible. Not even the most freedom-loving should see suicide through a lens of personal right because rights are shackled to responsibilities, and, for all of our individuality, we are not alone.

The gruesome practicalities of a suicide are one matter. Not all suicide attempts are successful, and the ones that fail are usually medical emergencies that everyone shares a partial burden in paying for. Further, all successful suicides have a unique feature in common. No one who succeeds in a suicide will be the one to clean up after it, and the mess will be precisely horrific. Finding and doing that hideous job will fall to others. (I used to know a big-city EMT who frequently had this task as part of his professional duties, and, even years later, he could barely bring himself to speak about this aspect of his job and the terrible impacts it had on him.)

Anyone unlucky enough to find the suicide of a loved one is sure to be traumatized beyond what most of us can fathom.

The scene of self-inflicted demise, the sickening realization of the sight, the incomprehensible horror—these will become the source of their most enduring nightmares for the remainders of their lives. This same pain, grief, shock, and utterly incomprehensibility will spread like cracks in shattering glass throughout the victim's social network. A suicide kills one and injures many. The assumption, then, that a suicide is something people do with their own lives, over which they have sole and unique power, is false.

In addition, most suicides are *unexpected* deaths, done in secret. While those intending to commit suicide may, in oblique ways, say their goodbyes, in most cases they rob their loved ones of any hope of a journey together toward accepting the impending death. Meanwhile, they set their closest loved ones up for an extremely difficult time—close family members make the top murder and wrongful-death suspects until the authorities can conclude a suicide was, in fact, a suicide. As if the suicide itself weren't hell enough for them.

Humans are extremely social animals, so we depend upon each other in immensely interconnected ways. Psychologically, we largely define ourselves by our connections with others. We see ourselves as we perceive other people see us. Through the social lens more than any other, we judge ourselves and arrive at our own sense of esteem. We are largely the people who love us; and the people who love us are, in turn, partly ourselves.

Hence, while you may have an inherent right to choose to end your own life, you cannot ethically do so privately. To kill yourself does more than just ending your own life; it takes away something deeply personal from those who love you and burdens them with a curse. It is not merely to perform an act upon yourself, upon a life you feel you own. You cannot make the decision to end your own life without harming those who love you, and while you may not owe anyone the continuance of your suffering for their benefit, you do at least owe them a clear explanation and a chance to talk you out of it or accept it. The ethical barrier to taking your own life is therefore far higher than many assume, and it is composed of each of us and what we mean to each other.

These ethical barriers to suicide, however, do not apply to death with dignity. Circumstances matter. The conditions that would justify a death with dignity are grim, but they are medically assessable facts. Moreover, the decision to die with dignity is in almost all cases likely to follow long conversations with loved ones, justifying to them why you need to take yourself from them in light of those hard facts. Should I receive a diagnosis warranting an ethical intentional end to my life, my family and I will have the opportunity to wrestle with the facts as they are. Their hard reality will leave no lingering doubts. Life after a suicide, on the other hand, provides more than the usual share of grief while burying the bereaved under a mountain of inconsolable what-ifs.

These distinctions clarify the ethical differences between death with dignity and suicide. In a death with dignity, the reasons for the death at its center are likely to be unpleasant but objective facts that are not present or not known in other suicides. Few serious ethicists would condone a death with dignity except in cases combining the worst conditions with no realistic hope of recovery. When these conditions aren't present, as in many suicides, the possibility of remedy is altogether too realistic and pertinent to admit a final solution.

Ethical Vegetarianism

Our difficulties in facing death may also contribute to challenging controversies ranging beyond the obvious ones, and these can have a significant impact on how we live our lives. Perhaps surprisingly, for example, the principled avoidance of eating meat is another topic of great ethical concern that depends upon our fears of death and dying, and it is one that may be misguided by our tendency to exaggerate those fears.

Before wading into it, the debate about ethical vegetarianism is a *very* complicated debate with many difficult factors that bear upon it. Despite its complexity, there are many very intelligent people on both sides of the question who feel the matter is settled beyond serious debate. Given that human beings can survive, often quite well, as vegans (with some supplementation like vitamins B12 and some short-chain homologues of vitamin K2), ethical vegetarians conclude that it is less ethical to farm and kill animals for human food than to rely essentially upon a plant-based diet.

Because this debate is so ethically fraught, let me make it clear what I am and am not doing. I will not present any other reasons for skepticism of ethical vegetarianism, though I have several. I also am not making the case that eating meat is more ethical than keeping a plant-based diet. It may be; it may not be. I don't know. I do not intend to express skepticism about plant-based diets themselves. My goal is to do nothing more than question one of the pillars upon which the ethical vegetarian platform rests. I just want to convey that we must be cautious in our reasoning on this topic because our moral intuitions are likely to be distorted by our own exaggerated fears of death and dying. (Though it's technically irrelevant, the reader may want to know that I say this as a former vegetarian who, despite wanting to accept it, never could quite convince myself of the *ethical* arguments for vegetarianism. I was even completely vegan for a few months in the effort.)

In particular, there is no reason for us to wade into the related debate over ethical farming practices. Industrial farming and slaughtering practices bring their own level of ethical weight to the discussion about plant-based diets given the *current* realities of meat production, but those are matters removed from the issue of death and dying. Nothing we will discuss reduces the imperative on ethical farming and slaughtering practices. We will not be getting deeply into it, but to say satisfactory practices of these kinds cannot exist in principle is a point of view that may not fully appreciate the realities surrounding both life and death.

There are reasons to doubt the conclusion that vegetarianism is *certainly* more ethical than other dietary arrangements and to feel those reasons given in its support have been reached too hastily. One reason for my skepticism is that there may be a general overestimation of the ethical failure constituted by killing animals for food. This poor assessment arises from our tendency to overestimate the suffering attendant to death and dying.

To get into the discussion, consider the impact upon the ethical arguments for a plant-based diet made by removing the one idea that death and dying represent some pinnacle of suffering that sentient creatures can experience. We need not even compare deaths—say, like those caused by intentional and collateral damage from the large-scale farming of plant-based foods required to sustain vegetarian populations—to immediately recognize that the entire substance of the ethical vegetarianism debate changes. Indeed, it mostly falls apart. If we exaggerate the suffering involved in slaughtering animals for food (because of our own inflated fears of death and dying), then there are serious reasons to hesitate with the judgment that plant-based diets are ethically superior, and especially that they are obviously so.

No matter how unpleasant the fact may seem, animal life requires death. This is a dry point but a fine and deep one. Your continued existence requires the death of countless living things and will from the moment you were born until you die.

Living things die, of course, but that's only the beginning of it. Life, in its most basic description, is matter organized to gather resources from the environment so it might make something like copies of itself. Resources are limited, though, and other living things need them too. Biologists would call this a naturally occurring "selection pressure."

Natural selection at its barest is little more than the explanation that, under competitive circumstances for raw materials, that which is better at gathering resources and copying itself will make more copies. Among the chemical resources needed to live, all animals require organic material to recycle into their own bodies. As life concentrates organic material, living things are one of nature's richest and most efficient sources of the raw materials to enable other life. So, life evolved to eat life. The pitiless universe will never shed a tear over the rather cruel certainty that the typical fate of the animal is to eat and then, eventually, be eaten.

The ethical vegetarian recognizes this fact and also that plants are a living thing redolent with organic materials. Their point about the inherent cruelty of diets that include meat does not fail to appreciate that nearly all life requires death; instead, it follows directly from recognizing that not all deaths are created equally. The belief goes that the deaths of sentient animals generate more suffering than those of less sentient creatures, and those generate more than the deaths of plants. There may be much truth in this observation, but it can easily overlook the standard of care that Nature provides to the majority of her animal children. Nature is said to be red in tooth and claw—and black in decay—for a reason.

Imagine yourself for a moment to be a gazelle with the good fortune to have been blessed with a clear choice and the reasoning to ponder it. Would you choose to die at the claws and teeth of a pride of devouring lionesses, in debilitating sickness resulting from an infected injury, in slow starvation in a lean season or dehydration in a dry one, or at the mercy of a hunter's bullet to the head? Choose one. It requires very little thought to appreciate that it isn't cheating to call the bullet a "mercy."

The bullet can be seen as a mercy because it reminds us that the total amount of suffering in dying can be quite high and yet can be rendered quite low. Wild deaths are frequently gruesome affairs that domestication—even when it ends in eventual slaughter—almost uniquely avoids. Accounted by the individual head, domestication and slaughter can minimize animal suffering in ways Nature rarely can. The more difficult question is how much suffering our farming practices induce in aggregate, given that we raise and slaughter enormous numbers of animals that never would have lived and died unless for our own consumption. Our compassionate intuitions may mislead us by imagining ourselves bred and raised in captivity specifically for the purpose of being slaughtered in the end for another species' food, but the animals we raise for food are unlikely to feel any such dread—a crucial difference between them and us.

As animals being farmed for their meat are also not being hunted to extinction, the ethical vegetarian's argument depends on more than suffering, then. It also hinges upon the sanctity of life. Is sentient life itself good?

If sentient life is good in itself, at least when life is good for it, then the ethical argument for a plant-based diet becomes far harder to make. Farming large numbers of animals in the relative peace of domestication creates an otherwise unrealized opportunity for a great deal of life in remarkable tranquility (assuming ethical farming practices, which are a separate concern). You may even notice it is precisely what we hope for most dearly for ourselves. Slaughter with even the merest attention to ethics, which we should exceed as much as we can manage, provides a death vastly superior to what most wild animals will endure, one (except in rare cases) only outstripped by the comfortable, highly domesticated deaths we hope for ourselves and our pets. If sentient life living the good life is good, ethically farming animals for food creates a lot of it.

On the other hand, without the assumption that sentient life is good in itself, the question reduces to a rather cool assessment of relative merits of diets and what goes into them. The debate collapses to one of balancing the costs, including net suffering, of animals raised for food against the benefits. We should weigh the degrees to which human and other domesticated animals' health and life satisfaction outcomes can be improved considerably by consuming certain quantities of animal products (but not necessarily others). If those benefits outweigh the costs, then the ethical vegetarian argument needs a different pillar. Given that the amount of suffering in death is exactly zero and in farming and slaughter can be minimized possibly to be quite low, it is plausible that the moral stance against diets including meat is exaggerated.

The problems driving ethical vegetarianism are unlikely to

be those they claim. At first blush, it seems to be believing death is inherently a very bad thing. Death is not suffering, however, and it is inevitable. Death on its own, then, shouldn't be the horror driving people away from eating meat. It isn't even the total amount of suffering involved in slaughtering vast numbers of animals for our own consumption. No one has ever heard a sane ethicist make a serious case for reducing the total suffering on Earth by murdering all sentient animals at once and having done with it, even though such a genocide would *end* suffering until it could evolve again, thereby possibly reducing it greatly in the long run.

What ethical vegetarians find so objectionable isn't really death; it's being complicit in an intentionally *caused* death. We do not farm animals wantonly, however. We do it to *feed people* (and other animals). It's less suffering that they want to reduce than having a sense of blood on their own hands.

There are a couple of loose ends to tie up before leaving this tricky topic. One surprising concern is that some will feel a similar case applies to eating human beings, which reveals the kind of moral imbecility usually reserved for complete academic detachment or the blinkers of zealotry. Pardon the disgust of the topic and the tedium of addressing the painfully obvious, but we do not eat human beings because we have relationships with them. All living human beings derive their humanity from their relationships with others, which begin during gestation. You'll notice immediately we feel the same for our beloved pets. We tend not to eat our pets, even when they are an animal routinely farmed for food, because we have imbued them with social meaning. These taboos are worth enforcing in all but the most extreme cases of need because they connect directly to what it means to be human.

Another issue concerns the increasingly realistic possibility of producing lab-grown meat. If we have lab-grown meat, the dietary ethics question becomes much more finely nuanced because there will be *no* need for any suffering by a living animal raised and then killed for its meat. On the other hand, there will be far fewer animals living in the relative comfort of domesticity (implying that widespread use of lab-grown meat may be a moral failure against the intrinsic value of life if it prevents the lives of large numbers of ethically raised and slaughtered food animals). So long as we do not see those lives as their own moral good, lab-grown meat shifts the debate over dietary ethics to finer practicalities, like the micronutrient profiles of raised versus lab-grown meat. (Living things are complicated, after all.) The rest would fall to ethically dry concerns like relative costs, if matters of taste can be concluded to be ethically irrelevant.

As lab-grown meat becomes widely available and affordable, the ethical discussion about the consumption of animal products will change significantly. In the meantime, however, we shouldn't be so hasty to conclude that plant-based diets represent moral virtue on the overly simplistic assumption that slaughter represents unconscionable suffering.

The Remedy

Our fears of death and dying are likely to be exaggerated, and they can mislead us in our ethical controversies—death with dignity, suicide, and consuming animal-based foods. Perhaps the main part of the reason they are so exaggerated, however, is the reason they are also truly terrifying. It isn't necessarily our own deaths, or even ourselves dying, that chills us; it's the fear of the deaths of those we love.

This fear is considerable and legitimate, and it serves not only as a point of discussion on fears related to dying but is the motivation driving the thesis of this book: the opportunity we each have for happiness and connection while we live. The fear of our loved ones dying, and knowing simultaneously that we are a loved one to each of them in return, is a truly haunting one.

As it is something even more terrible to contemplate than our own deaths—that some day your partner, your children, or, worse, your parents, will get *that call* about you—we simply tend not to think about it, and we often run from the fact when it crosses our minds. Take a moment now, if you're up to it, to consider it, and don't run from it.

There is no escaping the grief associated with the death of a loved one, absolutely none. To love is to grieve eventually, unless you are "lucky" enough merely to die before it seizes you, in which case you will be the cause of the same grief in others. Because we will experience the pain of bereavement, we know its anguish, and because we care, we dread that we, too, will one day be its cause. Thus, even if we are so fortunate as to live an easy and pleasant life—to avoid injury, sickness, poverty, and misfortunes of every other sort—a human life is guaranteed a certain measure of unavoidable grief.

The nearest we have to a remedy for grief is the realization that just as we wouldn't wish it upon our loved ones, so they do not wish it upon us. The suffering of mourning may be unavoidable, but it is rarely intended. Though the vaccine it provides is merely partial, we can prepare—practically and emotionally—for the deaths of those we love by admitting the facts of mortality to ourselves and changing how we live. In this way, death reveals a tremendous opportunity to live differently, and better.

ACCEPTING DEATH

People grow a lot when they are faced with their own mortality. I learnt never to underestimate someone's capacity for growth. Some changes were phenomenal. Each experienced a variety of emotions, as expected, denial, fear, anger, remorse, more denial and eventually acceptance. Every single patient found their peace.

—Bronnie Ware, from "Regrets of the Dying"

No one promises life will be easy. In fact, great suffering is all but guaranteed along the way, but life can be sweet and fulfilling. In all of the moments not fated to be miserable, we have the opportunity for happiness, and to share it with others. Even in the darkest hours we shall ever get to endure, there's the chance for perspective. Dreaded, welcomed, or merely as a way to better inform what time we have, we march unceasingly toward our own deaths, and we call the way we experience the march "living." Your life will mean more from the first instant you realize how fleeting and thus precious it is, and the more clearly you can remember that fact, the more pronounced the effect will be.

We have essentially two choices: we can go on living in the denial of death by embracing some kind of immortality story, or we can accept death for what it is and live differently. Living differently ultimately means living better, and it requires facing death for what it is. Living with a robust acceptance of death is a doorway to a unique opportunity to a happier and more fulfilling life.

It is not easy to accept death. The terror of death is immensely powerful, and the invitation to adopt immortality stories to keep it hidden is incredibly seductive. To accept death means to reject the temporary comfort in that invitation.

Facing death requires the courage to put away our vanity and our fear and sit face-to-face with the terror of death until it delivers no more torment. Accepting death requires some determination and the bravery to endure discomfort. To accept death you must, for as long as it takes, fixate dispassionately on the plain, unadorned truth—that you will die.

Once you can accept your death for what it is, you'll find you have access to happiness that you have ignored throughout your life. You will, for instance, immediately realize just how much time and how many opportunities you have been wasting. And for what? Whatever the answer to that question might be, most of us take it in exchange for a mountain of probable regrets that will come with not having done it sooner. We nearly all accept death in the end unless it takes us completely by surprise, but the trick is accepting death with enough time left to do something with what remains of our lives.

Accepting death is what we must do, then, and we should as soon as we are able. The question is how to do it.

Accepting your own death is little more than a matter of getting beyond the fears and embracing that your time is truly limited. That doesn't make it easy, though. Facing death and accepting it are not for the faint of heart.

You must calmly remind yourself repeatedly that you will die. There is no other way. You must contemplate your own death and what it means, and you have to do it over and over and over again. As you do it, you will be tempted by immortality stories, and these you must reject, or at least set aside. There can be absolutely no pretense, no hope laid in any assumption you cannot be sure of—and all you can be sure of when it comes to death is that *you will die*. You have to keep doing this, enduring all it brings up in you, until you accept death. There simply is no other way. None at all. The fact is, you will die, and that's it.

The process will be one of trial and tears as you contemplate how much you have to lose and what it means to you; it is one of frailty and setback, of coming to appreciate your smallness and powerlessness; and it may take months, or even years. If you cling to a powerful immortality story, like those provided by religion, undertaking this process may not even be possible unless you can at least set it aside, and that requires fierce, even ruthless honesty and an enormous amount of courage. All the while, you can expect creeping anxieties, tension, and malaise as various dreads manifest. If you catch them, they'll seem silly, but until you do, they'll pull you back into denial.

For most of us, sheer pretense is all that stands between us and the real terror of death. It isn't death itself that we truly fear, and it isn't dying. We believe our immortality stories to conceal a deeper dread from ourselves, the fear that we have lived life all wrong. The most common remorse people feel as death creeps toward the door is that we cared about the wrong things and thereby misused the time we had while we had it. The most pressing fear of death is that we, in our own arrogance and ignorance, are pissing away our one life—that we are wasting our one opportunity to connect with what really matters. As you contemplate your own death, you will feel this like you never have before, and you must endure it until you understand it viscerally.

If you get that far, then you have just gotten started. We delude ourselves with immortality stories that let us deny death, and we quell naive existential dread by turning an eye toward legacy, the desire to leave a mark. So we misuse our time. The impassive facts of entropy are an uncomfortable promise that legacy is only a temporary comfort. There, when the thought occurs to us, as it sometimes will, lies true existential dread, and it too must be overcome before we can claim to have accepted death. Facing it requires the same as facing death, although the feeling is different: endure an honest examination of extinction, and do it over and over again, until it no longer induces despair or nihilism and gives the gift of poignancy.

Succeed and you will realize that our lives still matter despite the eventual annihilation of everything meaningful. There is only one way to make such a realization, however, and so there is only one way to accept death. You must recognize that whatever matters must matter *now*, or at least soon. Overcoming existential dread realigns our priorities to the present and the near future. The obvious antidote to these problems is to stop pretending, find what makes your life worth living, and live it.

Hard though it may be, the terror and dread associated with our own deaths is the easy part, and in truly accepting death, it is also just the first part of the challenge. In the barest consideration possible, we all get the same lot, regardless of our choices: to live until we don't live any longer. Life is making it to an end we cannot avoid, and living is filling the space between with things worth feeling and doing. With our loved ones, though, it is completely different. We will watch some of them die and live on to remember.

If you have never stared into the abyss and want to, I can tell you where it is and how to look, and to accept death fully, you must look sooner or later and gaze into its depths for a long time. It can be found in mere minutes by contemplating the premature death of anyone that you truly love. To imagine waking up tomorrow to find out unexpectedly that you will have done so without one of the people who mean the most to you is to peer into a chasm in your psyche that cannot be filled.

It may not be possible to face the full reality of death without having truly loved first. The full story of the terror of death is one written almost entirely in the language of love. Love brings us to death, and death reflects back for us the meaning of love—and thus of life. In that reflection, we can also see ourselves sleepwalking toward horrible shock that will compound our impending grief. We can use this view to wake up to the opportunities we share with those we love, and we can do it before it's too late. The fear of our grief is like a fog that keeps us from seeing the importance of love, and that it is important *now*.

Often, our first attempt to reckon with the death of a loved one arrives with the grief of experiencing it. It isn't exactly that we don't realize our loved ones will die while we still enjoy their company; it's that we never let ourselves expect that their deaths are coming. Thus we frequently contemplate the full impact of death only in the torment of grief, when it is too late to do much about it.

Here again, then, we meet two choices. We can willingly face the reality of death in those we love, or we can wait for it to come to us, trampling. If we live and wait long enough, someone very dear to us will die, bringing the point home as gently as a lightning strike. Or we can prepare ourselves. We can harness the power of our imagination and will and take ourselves to the point at our own speed and in manageable doses. That is, we can face death by choice or we can wait until we have no choice.

We have an opportunity, for instance, to prepare for the possibility that we will have to leave "the party" sooner than we would. The details attendant to a funeral, the arrangements, the expense, the unanswered questions, the unsaid things, mementos—these are all matters we can choose to make easier for those who will grieve for us, and a little organization can go a long way, not just toward making a difficult time easier but also toward giving a last gift and reminder of our care. It's a matter worth the thought, and doing something with it can help us in our journey to accept our own deaths.

Accepting death makes life both more real and more precious—a long emergency, one pregnant with the best opportunities of our lives—and it softens grief. Mourning, though it will always be sorrowful, has the opportunity to take on a character of celebration of life and remembrance. Grieving becomes another part of life when we accept death, and even for all its sorrow, it need not be bitter.

The present moment is both fleeting and interminable, and it's all we've got, along with something close to a guarantee on a very short while ahead that fades as it stretches further into the future. The time immediately ahead of us, then, is always an opportunity. When we accept death, the opportunity we have in the present moment becomes that much clearer. Accepting death will require mourning our wasted hours, and it will cost us the pretense of our immortality, which as it dies takes with it some of our false hope and pride. Freed from those juvenile encumbrances, life after becomes a chance to do, to connect, to share, and to free ourselves of the wish to withdraw quite so much.

LIFE IN LIGHT OF DEATH

*The same view you look at every day, the same life, can
become something brand new by focusing on its gifts rather
than the negative aspects. Perspective is your own choice and
the best way to shift that perspective is through gratitude, by
acknowledging and appreciating the positives.*

—Bronnie Ware, from *The Top Five Regrets of the Dying*

There are no do-overs. You can try again next time *in* life, but
you cannot *on* life. Life is, as they sometimes say in the South, a
"one-time good deal." If you're going to get it right, you have to
get it right the first time.

This thought may evoke a sense of pressure, even dismay—
what if you *don't* get it right? How, in fact, could you? It's your
first time! Any immortality story that gives us another go, say
reincarnation, seems to take the edge off, but that's why those
stories are so seductive despite being so implausible.

Adopting immortality stories is what we're trying to avoid by facing and accepting death. Rather than adopting immortality stories, we want to take on a *mortality* story, and that demands that we rephrase the question. *How can we get life right the first time?* The answer must lie in how we focus our priorities onto what matters and use our time to attend to them.

It isn't so bad. Most of us have plenty of time to figure things out, and mistakes are nothing more than learning opportunities. How we use our time is what will make the difference, and here we face a double opportunity. We can make better use of our limited time, and we can learn how to see the moments of our lives fundamentally differently.

One of the most enduring mistakes in living is believing our lives are what we do when we're done with everything else. If I can just finish this work day, I can get back to my life. I just have to run these errands, do that for the kids, finish waiting in line at the post office (again!), get the groceries, drive home, make dinner, eat, clean the kitchen, walk the dog, pay the bills, return a few emails and then—at long last—life can begin, if it ever gets the chance. We believe life is what happens when nothing *has* to be done, except something else *always* has to be done and always will. We spend our lives with a never-ending belief that we have time, and frustrating monotony is all we get for it.

Everything we do is life. Everything. Even the boring stuff. *Especially* the boring stuff. Every moment of our lives are moments in which we live, or, to follow the poets, in which we have a chance to live, if only we will see it and seize it. We often fall into the trap of searching for "ourselves" by turning ourselves into a thrilling protagonist and then casting around for a perfect narrative that tells our story. Our lives *are* our story, already. Stop looking for your life outside of your life! Make the life you live fulfilling instead.

The easiest way to recognize the moments of our lives for what they are—moments of our lives—is to realize that sooner or later we run out of them. Everything we do is life, and every moment is an opportunity in which we can live. To reckon with death is to realize this simple fact, and it's an invitation to stop waiting to live, to live *now*.

We can gain perspective on our everyday moments by using the certainty of our deaths as a kind of mirror. Imagine reflecting upon life as if from your own deathbed. First, only imagine that you have just discovered you, as you are right now, have but a few hours to live and are in no state to do much more than think. Look back at your life thus far, weighing remorse and regrets against moments of happiness. What do you realize? What would you change? Think for a minute.

Now, what *will* you change?

Repeat the experiment, this time changing it. Don't imagine being on your deathbed as you are now, but pretend you're looking back at this moment from a deathbed that you will lie upon some decades in the future. You cannot change the life you have already lived—that cost is sunk—but you can change the life you'll live between now and the first moment it becomes too late. What suddenly matters more? What less?

Again, what will you change?

Such a thought experiment, a *deathbed contemplation*, is a chance to remember what matters. That perspective can inform how you can live more fully in the time that you have left. It will not give you a full picture of what life means, the opportunities that lie within it, or how you should live, but it can provide useful pieces of the puzzle.

In the long, backward view of a deathbed contemplation, certain aspects of life take on more meaning and others take on less. Peak experiences, those in which life seemed at its best or worst, seem to stand out, though their importance may fade into the background of the rest of life. "Buy experiences, not possessions," is sage advice with growing popularity, but cultivating love, relationship, connection, family, and passion is wiser still. What will matter to you when you're on your deathbed? Will it be having had experiences or having those nearby with whom you grew by sharing those experiences with them?

We can see clearly that how we spend our lives matters. It's hard, for example, to imagine lying there in your final hours pleased with yourself for obsessively checking Twitter five times a minute, hoping for that magical moment when it finally pays off. The same is true of "the treadmill of a work existence." Time invested in deepening the most treasured relationships of our lives and in pursuing work and passions that make life feel worth living, on the other hand, feels immediately justified. The lessons are clear—sometimes life is great; sometimes it isn't; some suffering is worth it in the long haul; meaning in life is near to hand; and what we do with our time *matters*, if only to us and those closest to us.

These are lessons worth learning about ourselves and the lives we lead, even if they aren't the whole story. They define something of the big picture for our lives and meanwhile help us focus on the kinds of details that make a difference. The arguments we should be willing to have with each other, and the things we argue about, for example, seem to change completely when we keep the view from our deathbeds in the backs of our minds. Bickering with a partner seems particularly pointless, and getting into another hostile political argument with a stubborn parent seems to miss the whole point. Spending yet another year waiting to take your kids to see the ocean for the first time, and not because you can't afford it, starts to lose whatever rationale it ever seemed to have.

A deathbed contemplation refocuses priorities. Because we cannot change our past and must accept it for what it is, the information a deathbed contemplation imparts is always of opportunity. The lesson is to live a little differently in ways that foster a better life over time. It changes how we connect with each other, raise our children, balance work and the rest of life, and seek our passions. It teaches us to cast off our pretenses, insecurities, and vanities. It has the power to change our lives, and it should be considered a crucial ingredient in making a life well-lived. The desire to foster our closest relationships and encourage other connections to grow closer takes on a particular salience that's all but impossible to deny, and the calls to generosity, kindness, and love are almost overwhelming. As for our passions, an imagined view from the end will drive us to seek them, and it will help us find that we often engage with many of them specifically to share them, together with the joys and fruits we are able to draw from them.

The exercise is, of course, imperfect. All a deathbed contemplation can do is inform our perspective, giving us a few glimpses of life that we too seldom take. Between now and those terminal moments from which we may one day look back are many, many moments of ordinary life. There are challenges to be met, work to be done, and the hard fact that most of our lives' moments will be thoroughly mundane. Those moments add up, one way or another, but they are invisible from a deathbed contemplation, which can tell us very little about specific actions to take in any given moment. The imagined view from our deathbeds cannot tell us much about the small picture. It cannot tell us what we should do now, where we will want to be in five years' time, or anything about the chances we'll hit upon along the road.

It can also distract and confuse us. The glaring light of mortality can make it hard to see the point of tedium, like another forty hours this week at an uninspiring job, filing our taxes, or washing the dishes. It can diminish the inherent rejuvenating worth of relaxed downtime. It would be as much a mistake to put so much emphasis on the poignancies of life that we lose sight of the practical. Life may be too short, but it isn't so short that investing in making it livable loses its meaning. Appreciating the myriad comforts and conveniences that can make life more fulfilling, and the small and routine actions that enable them, needn't get lost in the romantic fog of too big a picture.

If you will, consider the contemplation a few more times, placing your impending demise at different points in your future. Imagine being on your deathbed a month from now. A year from now. A few years from now. In a decade. Fifty years from now (no matter how old you are). And five hundred years from now (medical science be praised). Take a few moments on each. Notice how your priorities change in each case, and appreciate the apparent paradox. Particularly, practical matters take on far more importance as we imagine ourselves to have more time. Attending dutifully to a budget, for example, or securing a stable place to live comfortably become *more* important, not less, the longer we have. The clear lesson is that attending to the practical adds value to life that shouldn't be ignored. The reason we should give thought for the morrow is that most of us have rather a lot of them ahead of us.

Having more time, then, means embracing more tedium, and that can be a drag on the quality of life. Even if we cannot find a way to enjoy tedium in itself, it can be appreciated as a means for improving the rest of life. The tricks are balance and perspective. At once we can see that we must balance the fun with the boring, the practical with the enjoyable, work with play, and solitude with companionship, and the longer we have ahead of us, the more each side of each of these balances must be attended to. We'll return to perspective and balance shortly, however.

For now, notice that a related question teaches similar lessons with different emphasis. If you could know the hour of your death, would you want to?

You may be surprised at how easily you can make a case either way. Knowing would make planning and prioritizing much easier, not least because it would give a sense of how much time there is to waste. Not knowing prevents having to confront a truth that, in almost any case, will seem disquieting. The question itself, however, is a mere sideshow to the way it highlights both how it impacts our lives that we do not know and how our lives would change if we did, differently depending on when our doom will arrive.

If you knew you had a long time yet to live, you would prepare for a long life in comfort and happiness, bargaining upon your remaining time and setting priorities accordingly. If you knew you had very little time left instead, you'd probably live indulgently for all that remains. If you knew your time to be somewhere in the middle, you'd seek a balance, hedging some bets and playing others.

Not knowing when we will die, while realizing it could be at any point, is harrowing. We cannot look at the lifespan that remains to us and plan with the kind of certainties knowing would bring. Managing the resulting discomfort requires chasing a difficult balance between fulfillment in both the near term and in the long, and it forces us to embrace uncertainty and to be forgiving enough with ourselves to admit mistakes and miscalculations. Statistics can give us some insights but few guarantees, and for those of us in the developed world, we currently have good reasons to believe we should plan to live into the middle of our eighth decade, the last of that time not in particularly good health, and that we shouldn't bet the farm on the prospect. Accepting death means living prepared for the end to come upon us soon without succumbing to the indulgences that would come with knowing that it will.

The question that haunts us all when we face death is on how we should spend our limited time, not in knowing how much of it we have. We can be certain that many moments in our lives will be boring, tiring, exasperating, or absolutely frustrating. We are assured of suffering and misery—pain, sickness, grief, loneliness, self-doubt, self-pity. All are attendant to any life lived. We also know there are ample moments for happiness, connection, and passion and opportunities to encourage each of these in ourselves and each other.

At "happiness, connection, and passion" is where we come to it, a life in light of death. Happiness is really *something*, maybe the one real something. It's also something we know we have the capacity for experiencing in our own lives and that we can help bring to others' lives. We derive a great deal of our happiness from our connections with others and from our passions—those things that, when we do them, truly make us feel alive and glad for the fact.

Positive psychology is the branch of psychology that is particularly interested in happiness. It seeks to answer questions like, What makes people happy? How do we achieve happiness? Why do we seek it?

One of the core aspects of happiness investigated by positive psychologists is a state of mind that they call flow. When we feel like we are working on something that interests us, that we possess the skills to do well with, that requires our concentration, and yet that challenges us—that is, when engaging with our passions—we experience flow. People self-report the highest levels of happiness and satisfaction with life while in states of flow. Remembering that our opportunity to engage with our passions is short should encourage us to invest more time in flow-inducing activities—work, play, or otherwise—because they are for each of us the kinds of things that make life feel well-lived.

And then there's connection. Our connections with other people are some of the most deeply satisfying experiences that we will ever have in our lives. We are who we see ourselves to be in those who we love, and we are therefore defined in part by the love that we give. Nothing bares the value of our connections to us like death does because it teaches that our best relationships are all briefer than we would wish them to be. Such is life as a highly social animal; people were made for each other.

Why? Well, death and extinction are not the only truly hard facts of human existence. There is a harder one still. Every one of us is ultimately alone. Because we are irredeemably alone, our connections with others prove far more important.

You may not feel alone, but you are. One of the quirks of conscious experience is that we all live entirely inside of our heads, even as we interact with the world and people around us. Our senses provide inputs, and our nervous systems work upon impulses generated from those inputs to feed us the only thing we ever experience: conscious experience itself. The barrier between our subjective experience of reality and reality itself is complete, and thus so is our separation from the minds of those we love. It is the dichotomy between the subjective and the objective, and because our only experience of the world is our own subjective one, we are separate in a way from everything and everyone else. Just as you cannot truly experience what it is like to be a butterfly, so you can merely pretend to know what it is like to be somebody else, even if your guess might be considerably better. We are born alone, we live alone, and in the end we die alone, and there's nothing to be done for it except to make our isolation irrelevant.

Each of us is trapped within the perfect prison of our own subjective experience, but we live in a world our senses detect, and we live alongside others, connecting with them as they navigate an identical doom. We connect by affection and touch, by deed and by word, all by which we share intention and generate an experience in which we can enjoy companionship. The space we share with others is the only thing on Earth with the potential to make it not matter that we are each impossibly alone. It must therefore be honored and cherished for the treasure that it is, and it is nothing other than to love and be loved in return.

Our lives are intertwined with the lives of others, some nearer to us and some more remote, and we all face many of the same challenges. Whatever it is that makes a life meaningfully well-lived, much of it has to do with the quality of the connections we form with other people. To reflect upon death, then, is to realize just how important these relationships are, and it is a reminder to nourish them and enjoy them.

Time never feels more limited than when you suddenly realize that you don't have enough of it. Life, for too many of us, sadly ends up being little more than a desperate chase from one fleeting joy to another and a sleepwalk toward misery in between, but it doesn't have to be. How we choose to live makes the difference. So does how we express ourselves in light of what we care about—or how we fail to do so while we have the chance. More than that, *who* we spend our time caring about matters, as do the ways in which we care.

LOCAL PURPOSE

It all comes down to love and relationships in the end.
That is all that remains in the final weeks,
love and relationships.

—Bronnie Ware, from "Regrets of the Dying"

What is the purpose of life?

We only pretend this is a deep or hard question, and it only seems hard because we pretend we will never die. Just staring for a few hours at the honest reality of death causes all of the mystery to drop away. The question is absurdly simple to answer, and the answer is so absurdly simple as to make you laugh. Don't be mistaken. There's no trick here. The purpose of life is *to live it.*

Okay, you'll insist. *Of course*, the purpose of life is to live it, but the heart of the question concerns *how* to live it well. To do that, we have to somehow manage to live our lives in a way that maximizes our experience and our ability to reflect happily upon it, given the constraints of our abilities, our communities, and human psychology. The answer isn't too hard to come by, however. We need rewarding activities, a measure of what we deem to be goodness, well-nourished relationships, and the opportunity to pursue what happiness we can find without impinging upon others' abilities to do the same.

Also, if we want to live well, we cannot forget that what we choose to do is identical to how we live our lives. Losing sight of this basic fact is among the chief deceptions of a distracted mind, and most of us are quite easily distracted.

We live our lives in every moment that we are alive, whether we like it or not, and so we can choose to *live* in every moment if we learn to choose it. We frequently hear that *everyone dies, but not everyone truly lives*, and that there is a consequential difference between *living life* and merely *existing through it*. These statements speak to our attitudes about life, and they are reminders that we have some measure of power over how we shape the lives we live.

We have some dispositional control over how we view our moment-to-moment experience, even when that experience seems hardly worth noticing. We call this dispositional control "mindfulness," and by learning to slowly and calmly pay attention to what's happening around you and how you are reacting to it—and doing so without applying moral judgments, like the kinds that involve the word "should"—you can begin to make the most of even those moments that seem to mean the least.

We have an opportunity to face even the dullest moments of our lives as though they are exactly what they are—precious moments of our lives—or we can miss that chance and see them instead as moments in which living must be deferred until later. If we do the second of these too often, then we may find ourselves looking back someday wondering what we did with our time in life while we had it. We will have succeeded in existing but missed the spark that we consider *living*. In that way, to say that the purpose of life is *to live it* takes on a vibrant and immediate meaning.

The mistake most of us make when thinking about purpose in life is getting too big. We want to find a universal answer fitting everyone but specific enough to feel like it conveys deep meaning. That's impossible, and we have a bad habit of confusing impossibility for profundity. Even if we narrow our focus just to our own lives, we still tend to think in grand themes in place of realistic ones. We lose perspective by casting ourselves as protagonists in immortality stories in which we envision making a grand impact in the broader world or finding ourselves on the right side of some great moral struggle, and so we overlook the fact that the purposes of our lives are very near to hand.

Our purposes of life are primarily local to us. They are grand mainly because they are grand *to us*. There is nothing wrong with our purposes in life being local ones. Local purpose in life is what's near and meaningful to each of us. It includes our connections with loved ones and engagement in our passions. It is intimacy. It's the will to work for the betterment of ourselves and others. It's everything that makes life worth living.

Your partners in life give your life local purpose. Your spouse. Your children. Your parents and siblings. Your closest friends. Your relatives. Even your acquaintances and your community, including your roles within them. The broader society that you find yourself a part of, and those things, small and large, that you do within it. The activities you love, and those you wish you had more time for. Your bucket list, if you have one. Anything you love to do and the people you love to share yourself with.

To endure what you must endure without shattering under its weight. To change what you can change and to accept what you cannot, and to learn to tell the difference. All of these give your life local purpose, and no matter who you are, they constitute the bulk of your purpose in life—*to live them*—no matter what.

To truly live life is to recognize that these local purposes should be fostered, not denied or ignored. Meaning in life is not diminished on the profoundly silly grounds that most of what gives life purpose is small enough to be well within your reach. Our task if we want happiness, then, is to retreat from the exaggerated and to realize that local purpose is most of the purpose in life.

It sounds so simple, and it is, whether you're an everyday anybody or a great shaper of history. Those we love, the passions we have, our capacity to enjoy them for ourselves and to share them with others—these are everything that make life worth living, both in the moment and upon later reflection. The greatest tragedies, really, are how easily our local purposes get lost in the march and milieu of daily life and how quickly we forget them when we forget how finite and precious our lives actually are. Locality of purpose allows us to extract as much meaning and contentment out of our lives as possible by refocusing our priorities toward what is close to us. Death helps make that vision clear.

If you find your purposes, then you can answer a bigger question for yourself. *What is the meaning of life?* Connect with your local purposes, and you'll know.

If we crave something larger, we can find solace in the fact that local importance contributes to something bigger than ourselves even without our trying. The net effect of humanity is bigger than any of us. It is at least as big as all of us together, and it may be bigger. The combined effect of all of us attending fully to our seemingly little local purposes, grand only to ourselves, has a far greater effect overall. Our aggregated small efforts make great differences that reach across societies and generations, creating the very kinds of grand purposes of legacy that we long for and yet need only play a small part in producing.

We are small, then, and that's some comfort. We will die and will be forgotten, and that's more comforting still. Our impermanence contains a perverse freedom. In the grand scheme, what we do *doesn't* matter much. This is a lesson that can be quite freeing, but it is also profoundly constrained. To analyze this thought carefully shows that it isn't an invitation to selfishness, wantonness, or carelessness. What we should reject, however, isn't the belief that what we do matters; it's the value of the insidious notion of *the grand scheme.*

Most of us will not be remembered for more than a couple of generations after our deaths. Some, in fact, are tragically forgotten while they still live. Eventually, however, we will all be gone—all of us, humanity itself—and a distressing notion like being forgotten itself will become meaningless, a category mistake on the remorseless reality that there will be nothing relevant left to remember. It's sobering, and it forces us to reconsider our purposes in life and the ways in which we live. It brings our attention nearer, and it focuses it upon what really matters.

What matters, then? Ask yourself, knowing you will die.

Much of what came to mind is close to you, isn't it? *Did I make time for my passions? Did I connect with the people who make my life worth sharing? Did I give and receive love while I could? Did I do good or cause unnecessary hurt? Did I waste my time or use it well?*

Far from things not mattering at all, what we do matters

more where things matter at all—near to hand and nearer to heart. What we do with our lives really does add up, and its impact always hits hardest closest to home. We can, and do, make our environments better or worse; we nurture or injure our fellows, especially our children, who will inherit the world from us; we give love and support or cause pain and neglect in those we love; we make small decisions that, in aggregate, shape our cultures and societies, and thus many lives, for better and for worse. It all matters because it matters *to someone*, whether there's a Heaven to keep score or not.

We have such choices available to us, and we have the capacity to recognize that our choices matter, just in ways close to us. We therefore have the chance to realize the importance of the small but real actions we can take to improve our situations, and those of others near us, in ways that are likely to be lasting for the little whiles that they have meaning. Thus we can free ourselves from struggles that are ultimately misguided or trivial. And we can let go of desperation about the grand scheme, freeing ourselves from the weight of guilt and unrealistic expectations.

We all want a satisfying sense of purpose in life. Satisfaction with life and the capacity to help other people dear to us achieve it are the great human purposes. It seems strangely dissatisfying that our purposes are local to us, but their nearness makes them more poignant, not less. It's hardly more complicated than that most meaning in life is found in the activities and people we care most about, especially the people.

If we ask the dying, they tell us that they often wish they had lived a life more true to themselves, fulfilling their passions, and they also regret not having connected more with their families and friends. Healthy, supportive relationships enable both of these wishes while strengthening the sources of deepest meaning in our lives, and loving bonds enable us to open safely to the vulnerability of being ourselves. In our intimate connections with loved ones, then, lies the source of much of what people frequently report to be most fulfilling in life, and we grow in the sunlight of love because we perceive and value our loved ones' esteem for us and want to be better for it.

Because we are so profoundly connected to those with whom we share love, our entire subjective universe hangs upon the precious strands of meaningful connections in our lives. The goodness contained in our closest connections also reflects back upon us, allowing us to find purpose and joy in helping them to find comfort, happiness, support, and success.

In many respects, we are the connections that we make and maintain with other people. We should cherish the mutual bonds of affection, care, and concern that define human relationships, for these are finite. Death will end them, and then not long after death will end their memory too. Because they are so finite and so precious, we must nourish the relationships we value and escape the ones that do us no good.

Working for the happiness and connection we have with those we love, in fact, may be the easiest way to achieve flow— that state identified in positive psychology with the most happiness and satisfaction in life. Seeking to help those we love feel loved, happy, secure, and connected to us is one of the easiest things we can do to achieve positive feelings, and it is therefore little wonder that connecting in love is one of the most valued experiences in people's lives. Truly, the more we give, the more we have.

Living life in light of death, then, carries with it a demand to live fully and yet with kindness, even a generosity of spirit in sharing what care we have to share. In the time we have, we have a chance to chase our dearest dreams, connect, and lift each other up whenever we can. Saying so, of course, is not to mistake living for hedonistic abandon or kindness for indulgence, by which we do no real favors, but a spirit of adventure and friendliness are impossible to deny when we realize we all will die and most will grieve at times to the limits of human endurance. We truly have no good excuses for excessive prudence, cruelty, selfishness, or meanness.

Before we die, we must therefore take risks of the right kinds and live courageously, fully, vulnerably, and openly, and before we lose our loved ones, we must find ways to connect and give and share. We must take time for our passions and share those, too. There are no do-overs; life surely is a one-time good deal; and there are good uses of our time. *Carpe fatum!* Seize your destiny. Live, love, and be only as afraid as befits the situation.

Anything we would regret having let pass us by must be considered seriously, especially when doing it takes us outside of our comfort zones—or even outside of ourselves. Our destinies are mostly what we make of them, and regrets can be minimized—but really only by realizing and doing something with the tremendous opportunities that life throws at us while we have the chance. Life is an incredible opportunity, and death makes it clear.

THE BALANCING ACT

There is nothing wrong with loving your work and wanting to apply yourself to it. But there is so much more to life. Balance is what is important, maintaining balance.

—Bronnie Ware, from *The Top Five Regrets of the Dying*

There is an important difference between regret and remorse. We bear remorse for things we did that we wish we hadn't, or that we wish we had done better than we did. Those failures we can atone for. We carry regret for those things that we did not do, knowing, if only in retrospect, we had the opportunity and didn't take it. Those we simply regret. The difference between remorse and regret is most stark when imagined from our future deathbeds. Imagined remorse urges us to live better, and imagined regret instructs us to live fully.

What regret and remorse share in common is a story of

opportunity to live a better life. For remorse, we have the chance to make up for it—to apologize, to reconnect, to do better, and to change our behavior to produce less of it. With regrets, we can live to minimize them by living more truly to ourselves while we have the chance and by being brave enough to take full advantage of the freedom that good health provides while it lasts. There isn't always tomorrow, and tomorrow isn't always a better day. There is some truth, however, in the old saying that you don't know what you have until you've lost it. A life lived in light of death is a life that honors our opportunities by making the most of them.

Because we can always do something in response to our remorse once we feel it, regret is the harsher of these two punishments of misspent time. One of life's most common regrets follows more or less directly from the equally common belief that there will always be more time. For most of us, we have many years left ahead of us, but lacking a guarantee, we cannot squander the chances we have now. Getting this wrong is a guarantor of considerable regret. Too many of us work too much or are too prudish to welcome joy that stands before us, and midlife crises and later miseries are the rewards for our hesitance.

On the other hand, neither can we be derelict in preparing for the years we will have down the road. Flying by the seat of one's pants is largely an indulgence afforded by youth, and, as anyone who has endured chronic pain or debilitation can tell you, age brings enough discomforts not to want to multiply them. Failing to prepare adequately for our futures, or for those of our children, will shower us with both regret and remorse when it comes to it, and neither of these bitter fruits of our own foolishness will admit much remedy by the time we feel them.

Death can tell us we must prioritize our time and live well, even if it does little to clarify the balancing act between now and later. Everything in life is a gamble that we make upon what economists call *opportunity cost* (the sacrifice of the opportunity to do something else with our time once we have done something with it), and learning to play the game well is done by playing. In fact, learning the game is part of the game. Of all the lessons we will learn along the way, there is little doubt that one of the most valuable is seeing that time becomes far harder to waste when seen in the light reflected by death. Appreciating that life is short and guaranteed to terminate enhances our sense of opportunity—in every one of life's moments—and our desire to do something with it.

A note must be made, however. Life is hard enough without making it harder by accepting an overbearing responsibility to live fully in every moment, to "waste" no time at all. Psychologically, it seems very valuable to have time that is merely downtime, maybe even distracted time from the other responsibilities of living. Even honoring our need to relentlessly pursue passions and invest in loved ones rapidly becomes exhausting unless yet another balance is struck. To get the most out of our lives, much easy-going levity, some meaningless indulgence, and plenty of unstructured, unpressured time is necessary. Not every moment should be poignant or heavy. Downtime can and should be taken, then, and it should be enjoyed without the weight of guilt. Finding a good life demands recognizing the value in letting some of our time just be time spent.

So, what constitutes spending our time well, then? We can draw some hints from three persistent and overlapping themes common to people who suddenly realize death is both imminent and unavoidable. When the veil we use to hide from death from ourselves is parted, we often see the lives we have lived in a completely new way. Whatever we see, it must hit us fairly squarely between our newly uncovered eyes because most of us are called to seek forgiveness, remembrance, and meaning. These are not themes that speak to feeling life was well-lived.

We want to feel forgiven, often for having misused our time; we want to be remembered, even if only by the strangers attending to us in our last moments; and we want to be assured our lives were meaningful. All three of these terminal priorities speak to the importance of human connection and having used our limited time well, and it is telling that, if our last moments come upon us unexpectedly, these are the matters that concern us most. It's fair to say that it must be far better to realize their value when we have years or decades to act upon them, rather than mere minutes imprisoned by whatever circumstances brought us to the final brink.

It cannot be reiterated enough. What we do with our time matters, if only to ourselves and those closest to us, and it is by working out what truly matters to us that we can live our lives most fully. To truly live well, it seems we must set aside our immortality projects and take our opportunity to connect with those who matter to us, do things that make a (local) difference, and pursue what we love.

In pursuing what we love, it is crucial to remember that we each are important figures in our own lives, and our passions matter. Have you ever noticed the reactions that people have when someone dies doing something that she loves doing? Amidst the loss and overwhelming grief, almost everyone touched by such occurrences makes remarks like, "at least she died doing something she loved." Our passions are integral to our views of what makes for a meaningful life—and even a good death. We owe it to ourselves (and to others) to engage as fully as we can with our lives' passions. Regrets over a life wasted on the meaningless and selfish vanities often stand out from the lips of the dying, but we cannot let the fear of this regret prevent us from living for ourselves.

Still, we cannot be too self-indulgent if we want to live well. Self-indulgent pleasure-seeking isn't satisfying, and it often turns to regret in the end, even when it doesn't generate remorse. While we certainly need to experience some joy, even sometimes self-indulgence merely for its own sake, it is possible to overdo it. One of the horrors commonly expressed by the dying is specifically the regret of having spent too much time on themselves and our their pleasures and not enough on making more meaningful uses out of their time. As with so many things, a balance is needed in our pursuits of pleasure, and some of our passions have to carry some kind of lasting weight. Our future selves, right up until the last one, will thank us dearly for attending to this balanced approach to living.

Living for ourselves seems to be done best, when not indulging in downtime or outright fun, while pursuing at least one serious hobby or activity that holds rewarding meaning for us. These activities occupy our time in ways that enrich both our own lives and the people we continually grow into being. They therefore create the opportunity to share something we find deep and meaningful about ourselves with those we love. Our interests make us interesting, and sharing what we learn, experience, and value is one of the most rewarding activities most of us engage with.

Whatever planning, patience, and preparations might be needed, we aren't blessed (or cursed) with an unlimited amount of time in which to do the things that will make our lives, and the lives of those we love, truly worth living. A good life demands a difficult balance between preparing for the future and living for the present. Spending a little time calmly appreciating that we each will die can help keep the importance of these demands in view.

At the crux of this intersection lies our working lives. We work in order to live, and yet we often let work consume our lives. In struggling to find balance, we want an assurance that, when we spend our precious hours laboring (often for little more than the money it provides), we aren't making a bad trade. The difficulty in finding a good work-life balance is that we usually have to spend rather a lot of our time working. Some of us—just some—are lucky enough to be able to make our passions into careers, to turn our hobbies into a rewarding and stable source of income. Most of us have to fit most of what we look most forward to in life around work, struggling between working to live and having the chance to feel like we are really living.

Our paid work enables our lives, and thus it pays for what has the potential to allow our happiness. On the other hand, it often is not how we would choose to spend our time unless we had to, and the realities of our working culture provide fewer options than many of us would want. Most of us, for instance, will never have the opportunity to choose to work three quarters as many hours for three quarters the pay, even if we determined such a state of affairs struck a better balance for our lives. Jobs are defined around completing tasks (often for other people who may care about them more than we do) and thus don't always provide options of that kind.

Still, there are few miseries like struggling for money. Money, or the lack of it, is one of the leading causes of domestic friction and broken relationships (John, George, Paul, and Ringo were romantically deluded when they sang, "All you need is love"). Our opportunity for happiness has to be financed in order to be experienced, and there's little joy to be had in a continually stressed march through life. The best we can do is attempt to find a balance that works for us and a means for enabling it.

Finding the right balance between work and the rest of life often hinges upon negotiating the tensions of competing needs and desires that reside in two overlapping universes: the need to earn enough money so we can live the lives we want and the need to work a job we'd rather not to earn that money. Compounding the struggle, much of the work we do is done on the behalf of those we love, especially spouses, aging parents, and children. The difficulty there lies in the harsh irony that work takes us away from our families, who we are in part working to support.

Part of that balance must also include working not only to enable our lives now but also for the benefit of our future selves. We'll do ourselves few favors by condemning our eventual retirement to destitution. The autumn and winter years come to every life not prematurely cut by unexpected tragedies, and strategies to make old age a fruitful, even joyous time of life are well worth the investment made by sacrificing some of our youth. We may only have *now* in which to live and act, but the people we will be in many nows to come will be thankful for our consideration. Both too much and too little work, then, are sources of remorse and regret near the end of our lives, and so yet again, the point proves that living well demands striking a balance between competing forces.

To be sure, there are ways around this problem, but they involve risks and sacrifices. For example, many people decide to work far harder than they otherwise would, carrying a ridiculous workload while living extremely frugally through their twenties, specifically so that they do not have to work as long, entering semiretirement far earlier than most of us can. The risks in this approach run in direct proportion to the likelihoods of failure and of dying too early to get to appreciate the effort. The sacrifice is most of one's free time and comfort during some of the healthiest and most fun years of life. Other options require other decisions and other trade-offs.

We have an uncanny talent for distracting ourselves with a discontented search for more. Most of us want more most of the time—more stuff, more love, more happiness, more success, more fame, more comfort, more food, more experiences, more excitement, more status, more sex, more money, more life— and we spend a considerable amount of our limited time made miserable by these unsatisfied desires. Remarkably, it isn't even that many of these pursuits are easily seen to be frivolous, transitory, or ultimately unimportant that makes us miserable. The desire for *more* always goes unsatisfied, so the pursuit is as vain as it is tiring. When we get this wrong we remain unsatisfied, and then we die.

Any approach to a work-life balance can be aided by a single change in disposition that makes even more sense in light of death: living relatively modestly. Our relentless and dissatisfying pursuit of *more* costs us more, too, and it isn't necessary. When you are about to die, it isn't likely that you will care whether you had a new car every year if having it took you away from your family twice as much as needed. Nice things, and enough of them, of course, can make life more comfortable or enjoyable, but there is no joy in them when working enough to afford them makes them a waste. Time is worth more when you know it is limited. Well, let me break it to you again. You are going to die.

Your time is limited.

How can we find balance in the moment, then? A highly relevant consideration is available by asking yourself the pointed question, *what would you give up for someone that you love?* Chances are, the answers that you can imagine giving to this question are quite dramatic. They're likely to include effectively every material possession that you have, some relationships, and potentially your own life. Each of those categories of sacrifice is an interesting point for reflection and engagement on what really matters to you, and how much.

Imagine going through your most precious valuables one by one and being asked to sacrifice them for the life (or just the benefit) of someone who you love dearly. It doesn't matter whether those things are precious to you because of monetary or sentimental worth, all that matters is that they are precious, that they are things, and that their worth is being compared against that of a loved one. Which of these would you sacrifice for the needs of those you love? What if it were merely for their whims? The answers you're giving are probably pretty amazing, and they can teach you that the relentless pursuit of *more* is a hurtful distraction.

Now place yourself in a harder place. What of *yourself* would you risk or give up for someone you love? Your future opportunities, your free time, your hobbies or passions, any damaging relationships, or even your life? The answers you come up with if you contemplate these kinds of questions seriously may surprise you, or they may unnerve you, or they may change your life.

One thing that your answers may reveal to you is just how important your dearest loved ones are to you. More than that, it can show you just how much you'd be willing to give up for their happiness. Is it really worth working *that* much overtime so you can fill an oversized house with exorbitant toys? And isn't it worth it to get out and make a decent living so your lives together can be easier, more comfortable, more fulfilling, burdened by less conflict, and filled with better opportunities? The way you answer questions like these can help you find your work-life balance.

Combined with the realization that their time alive is, like yours, profoundly limited, such an exploration also holds the power to be profoundly transformational. Why bicker with someone so meaningful, or maintain a petty feud or spiteful grudge? Why waste your brief time, or theirs, in that way if any other way is available? These questions are far harder to answer because all of their answers are bad.

Easier to see is the opposite: an awareness of just how valued your loved ones are to you and how important it is not to take them for granted. There's an opportunity to nourish a relationship in every moment that you have together with another person. Because of the intensity of the connections we have with our closest others, death and love act as mirrors that reflect one another. Tell people you love them and mean it; be there for them; let them be there for you. We get weird about love but don't have to. We can love someone with no strings, with no expectations, and we can simply give love for as long as we want to because it is ours to give. If you love someone, tell them so and show it, but, as Paul reminds the Corinthians in his first letter, love, when it is love, is not self-seeking. If love is free to be given, it also cannot be demanded.

When you realize that a person who is very important to you really will die, a person that you'd give almost anything for, the result is often an incredible desire to support that person's pursuit of happiness to the largest degree that doesn't dramatically diminish your own. It becomes as easy as breathing to wish kindness and comfort upon them, and it is just as easy to wish for their success and happiness. Finding ways to encourage and nourish those follows quite naturally, and (with just a little work) so can a discovery that through your love for them, their happiness often is your own as well.

That feeling is expansive. The moment you can feel it for your closest love, it also becomes easy to extend it to other people who are close to you. We all can easily desire the happiness of those who mean a great deal to us and find the capacity to delight in their happiness for its own sake, realizing life and joy are a temporary state of affairs that are best spent shared. Likewise, we can extend a feeling of goodwill that bends us toward compassion, encouragement, support, and kindness.

Amazingly, there doesn't seem to be any limit to the extension of this feeling once it is accessed. By starting with our closest loved ones and, perhaps through realizing that almost everyone is someone's closest loved one (and that a spirit of negativity and malice is unlikely to add anything good to the world), we can stretch this outward-directed feeling of love to essentially anyone. There needs to be no limit on how far we can extend the feeling of wanting the best for people—even our enemies, even people we hate. And here is where love triumphs over retribution. Even for our enemies, knowing that they will live, suffer, and die, we can find space to want the best for them despite the hurts they have caused. What we might call "Big Love," perhaps of the sort widely attributed to Jesus, or pursued in the meditation practice known as *metta*, can be glimpsed, even enjoyed, in the view provided by the mirror of death.

We need not be naive, of course. Wanting the best for our

enemies is not an invitation to toxic excesses of compassion, nor does it absolve the need for justice. Justice for all involved in discordant situations is a complicated process, to be sure, and it may even warrant separation, restraint, imprisonment, or violence. The cases in which these responses are warranted are easy to imagine and include preventing abuse, self-harm, criminal behavior, or greater violence. Caring for those we dislike can dissolve our hatred, still, and it can guide our sense of justice away from the surfeits of retribution.

Retribution, to make a point, must be treated carefully because we are naturally inclined to it. Studies repeatedly suggest that people are so prone to the retributive impulse that we will pay for the opportunity to exact it. The desire to do so is even intimately related to moralistic behavior, which can become frenzied when amplified by morally charged immortality stories that we use to deny death. Therefore, justice is surely easier to find when we aren't blinded by a morally driven desire for retribution.

We love best when we realize we will grieve our loved ones terribly should it be our part to bear it. Love and kindness are best spent generously, and opportunities to live, to love, and to share should be seized while the fleeting moments for them are available. The borders of where we can spend love and kindness, at least in principle, do not seem to exist. Certainly, it would be impossible in practice, in the ways we usually think of it, to love everyone—meaning to invest time in them—but that's merely a matter of practical application, not sentiment. There's no reason whatsoever not to wish the best for the wide majority of people, and to find the capacity to be happy with the simple notion that they are, in their own ways, flourishing.

As we draw our circles of connection nearer to ourselves,

the imperative to live and love fully grows in potency, and with it so does our capacity to draw upon it for ourselves. Closeness and vulnerability strengthen the love we give and all we derive from it, and so by giving love and kindness generously to those dearest to us, we find a wellspring of strength and positivity for ourselves. Best of all, this circle is virtuous. Extending love and kindness often leads others to do the same. The most direct way to realize the importance of being generous in love and kindness *now*, in this moment, is to realize we each will die and so the chance cannot last forever.

It may be that our humanity is most visible in the recognition of our inherent fragility. Each of us will die, ending a life that has an opportunity to be a wonder, if only by our own subjective estimates. Love seems deeply integral to making human lives into miniature wonders unto themselves, and of all of the vanities that we distract ourselves with in life, those that cause us to forget opportunities for love are perhaps the most tragic. Death, if we're brave enough to face it honestly, is one of the best reminders we have of the importance of love, which enriches all of the lives it touches.

THE END

Dear friend think as you pass by
As you are now once was I
As I am now, you must be
Prepare in time to come to me.

—Epithet on the tombstone
of Emma McCarter (1881–1906)

The deepest horror of death is that we want to ignore it until it's always already too late to do what it asks of us, to live and to love now and to give not a damn that all things are impermanent. Now—the present moment in which we each live—is both fleeting and interminable. It's also nearly all we've got, and it's always an opportunity. *Life* is an opportunity to live, to connect, to experience, to wonder, and to love, and it's often only visible for what it is when it's seen reflected in the mirror of death.

Choose to live bravely. Face your death and accept it. Love. Happiness awaits.

> *Love's not Time's fool, though rosy lips and cheeks*
> *Within his bending sickle's compass come;*
> *Love alters not with his brief hours and weeks,*
> *But bears it out even to the edge of doom.*

—William Shakespeare, from "Sonnet 116"

ACKNOWLEDGMENTS

There are dozens of people who directly helped to make this book possible, especially those who took the time to read the early manuscripts and give their honest appraisals, and I thank them all. This book is vastly better than it would have been otherwise, and thanks are due to every single one of them. I will only name two in particular, however, for their professional suggestions.

To Peter Boghossian, I owe tremendous thanks and for many reasons. He went in detail through two versions of the manuscript and, at each reading, provided feedback of tremendous worth. I hope I've done his suggestions justice. He was also continually supportive and instrumental in helping the book reach a much larger audience of readers who, in their turn, provided useful commentary and asked insightful questions.

To my publisher, Kurt Volkan, I also express my deep gratitude yet again, not least for taking a chance on a book this short with me. His commentary and questions also enriched the book considerably, and his support has been extraordinary.

Thanks also to everyone who has loved me and let me love them for teaching me the lessons that made this book possible in the first place. And, of course, I have to thank my wife, as should be evident in the text, but not the least for booking that first trip to Asia for me and putting up with the fallout.

NOTES

In the "Existential Horror" section, the *emotional priority theory*, mentioned near the end, is creditable to Michael Shermer.

The sentence "We live much of our lives, it has been said, merely waiting for the future to arrive with its potential for happiness, and it never does." in the "The Emergency" section paraphrases the language of Sam Harris in his talk "Death and the Present Moment," after which that section is also titled.

The statement in the "Denying Death" section claiming that witnessing breastfeeding also induces mortality salience is derived from a paper by Cox, Goldenberg, Arndt, and, Pyszczynski in *Personality and Social Psychological Bulletin*.

That fewer than 2 percent of people who believe Hell exists believe also that they will go there can be referenced in Hood, Hill, and Spilka, *Psychology of Religion*, p. 185.

In the section "The Fear of Death," the phrasing "becoming less than the meanest ghost" alludes to J. K. Rowling's *Harry Potter and the Goblet of Fire*.

Further down in the section "The Fear of Death," the phrasing "that the existential issue at the heart of death that bothered him most isn't so much that the party is ending but rather that it is most assuredly going on—though without you in it" paraphrases Christopher Hitchens from his memoir, *Hitch-22*.

The quoted phrase "the treadmill of a work existence" in the section "Life in Light of Death" directly quotes Bronnie Ware from "Regrets of the Dying."

In the section "Life in Light of Death," the sentence "If you know—and you do—that every person you care about will one day also get *that* phone call, and will suffer besides, then nothing makes sense to do but extend as much kindness as we can in the meantime." paraphrases Sam Harris in his "Death and the Present Moment" talk.

The characterizations of remorse versus regret in "The Balancing Act" are ultimately derived from Christopher Hitchens in his memoir, *Hitch-22*.

The statement in "The Balancing Act" that people who suddenly find themselves about to die demonstrate a call "to seek forgiveness, remembrance, and meaning" is derived from Matthew O'Reilly's TED talk, "Am I About to Die? The Honest Answer."

SELECTED BIBLIOGRAPHY

Barker, Dan, *Life-Driven Purpose: How an Atheist Finds Meaning* (Durham, NC: Pitchstone Publishing, 2015).

Beck, Julie, "What Good Is Thinking about Death?" *Atlantic*, 28 May 2015, http://www.theatlantic.com/health/archive/2015/05/what-good-is-thinking-about-death/394151/.

Becker, Ernest, *The Denial of Death* (New York: Free Press, 1973).

Boghossian, Peter, James A. Lindsay, and Phil Torres, "How to Fight Extremism with Atheism," *TIME*, 16 September 2016.

Boniwell, Ilona, Susan A. David, and Amanda Conley Ayers, eds., *Oxford Handbook of Happiness*, Oxford Library of Psychology Series (Oxford: Oxford University Press, 2014).

Brooks, Arthur C., "To Be Happier, Start Thinking More about Your Death," *New York Times*, 9 January 2016, http://www.nytimes.com/2016/01/10/opinion/sunday/to-be-happier-start-thinking-more-about-your-death.html.

Brown, Brene, *Rising Strong: The Reckoning, the Rumble, and the Revolution* (New York: Spiegel & Grau, 2015).

Brown, Brene, "The Power of Vulnerability," TED Talk [video], recorded June 2010, https://www.ted.com/talks/brene_brown_on_vulnerability?language=en.

Buettner, Dan, *The Blue Zones: Lessons for Living Longer from the People Who've Lived the Longest* (Washington, DC: National Geographic Press, 2008).

Byock, Ira, *Dying Well: Peace and Possibilities at the End of Life* (New York: Riverhead Books, 1998).

Cave, Stephen, *Immortality: The Quest to Live Forever and How It Drives Civilization* (New York: Crown, 2012).

Cave, Stephen, "The Four Stories We Tell Ourselves about Death," TED Talk [video], recorded July 2013, http://www.ted.com/talks/stephen_cave_the_4_stories_we_tell_ourselves_about_death?language=en.

Chandler, Len, "Keep on Keepin' On," (1964) on the album *To Be a Man*, Columbia Records, 1967.

Cherry, Kendra, "What Is Flow?" *Very Well*, 6 May 2016, https://www.verywell.com/what-is-flow-2794768.

Cho, Jeena, "How Doctors Die Differently," *Forbes*, 28 June

2016, http://www.forbes.com/sites/jeenacho/2016/06/28/how-doctors-die-differently/#3cf9bceba94d.

Christakis, Nicholas A., *Connected: The Surprising Power of Our Social Networks and How They Shape Our Lives—How Your Friends' Friends' Friends Affect Everything You Feel, Think, and Do*, reprint edition (New York: Back Bay Books, 2011).

Cohen, Chapman, "Monism and Religion" and "An Old Story," in *The Portable Atheist: Essential Readings for the Nonbeliever*, ed. Christopher Hitchens (Philadelphia: Da Capo, 2007).

Crowell, Steven, "Existentialism," *The Stanford Encyclopedia of Philosophy* (Spring 2016 Edition), ed. Edward N. Zalta, http://plato.stanford.edu/archives/spr2016/entries/existentialism/.

Cox, C. R., J. L. Goldenberg, J. Arndt, and T. Pyszczynski, "Mother's Milk: An Existential Perspective on Negative Reactions to Breast-Feeding," *Personality and Social Psychological Bulletin* 33, no. 1 (January 2007): pp. 110–122, http://www.ncbi.nlm.nih.gov/pubmed/17178934.

Csikszentmihalyi, Mihaly, Finding Flow: The Psychology of Engagement with Everyday Life, reprint edition (New York: Basic Books, 1998).

Csikszentmihalyi, Mihaly, *Flow: The Psychology of Optimal Experience* (New York: Harper, 2008).

Csikszentmihalyi, Mihaly, "Flow, the Secret to Happiness," TED Talk [video], filmed February 2004, http://www.ted.com/talks/mihaly_csikszentmihalyi_on_flow?language=en.

Dewall, C. Nathan and Roy F. Baumeister, "From Terror to Joy: Automatic Tuning to Positive Affective Information Following Mortality Salience," *Psychological Science* 18, no. 11 (November 2007): 984–990, available online at http://www.uky.edu/~njdewa2/DeWallBaumPsychScienceinpress.pdf.

"Doctor-Assisted Dying: Final Certainty," *Economist*, 27 June 2015, http://www.economist.com/news/briefing/21656122-campaigns-let-doctors-help-suffering-and-terminally-ill-die-are-gathering-momentum.

"Doctor-Assisted Dying: The Right to Die," *Economist*, 27 June 2015, http://www.economist.com/news/leaders/21656182-doctors-should-be-allowed-help-suffering-and-terminally-ill-die-when-they-choose.

Epicurus, "Letter to Menoeceus," curated at epicurus.net, http://www.epicurus.net/en/menoeceus.html.

Gawande, Atul, *Being Mortal: Medicine and What Matters in the End* (New York: Metropolitan Books, 2014).

Gawande, Atul, "Death and the Missing Piece of Medical School," Ideas.TED.com, 31 October 2014, http://ideas.ted.com/death-and-the-missing-piece-of-medical-school/.

Goldman, Emma, "The Philosophy of Atheism," in *The Portable Atheist: Essential Readings for the Nonbeliever*, ed. Christopher Hitchens (Philadelphia: Da Capo, 2007).

Gorgenstein, Dan, "How Doctors Die: Showing Others the Way," *New York Times*, 20 November 2013, http://www.

nytimes.com/2013/11/20/your-money/how-doctors-die.
html?_r=0.

Haidt, Jonathan, *The Happiness Hypothesis: Finding Modern Truth in Ancient Wisdom* (New York: Basic Books, 2006).

Haidt, Jonathan, *The Righteous Mind: Why Good People Are Divided by Religion and Politics* (New York: Vintage Books, 2012).

Harris, Sam, "Death and the Present Moment," talk, April 2012, https://www.youtube.com/watch?v=ITTxTCz4Ums.

Harris, Sam, *Free Will* (New York: Free Press, 2012).

Harris, Sam, *The Moral Landscape: How Science Can Determine Human Values* (New York: Free Press, 2010).

Harris, Sam, *Waking Up: A Guide to Spirituality without Religion* (New York: Simon & Schuster, 2014).

Henig, Robin Marantz, "A Life-or-Death Situation," *New York Times Magazine*, 21 July 2013, http://www.nytimes.com/2013/07/21/magazine/a-life-or-death-situation.html.

Hitchens, Christopher, *Hitch-22: A Memoir* (New York: Twelve, 2011).

Hitchens, Christopher, *Mortality* (New York: Twelve, 2014).

Hood, Ralph, Peter Hill, and Bernard Spilka, *Psychology of Religion: An Empirical Approach*, 4th ed. (New York: Guilford Press, 2009).

Johnson, Carolyn Y., "The Sobering Thing Doctors Do When They Die," *Washington Post*, 6 June 2016, https://www.washingtonpost.com/news/wonk/wp/2016/06/06/how-doctors-really-die/.

Kubler-Ross, Elisabeth, *Death and Dying: What the Dying Have to Teach Doctors, Nurses, Clergy, and Their Own Families*, reprint edition (New York: Scribner, 2014).

Kuhl, David, "Facing Death: Embracing Life," *Canadian Family Physician* 51, no. 12 (December 10, 2005): pp. 1606–1608, available online at http://www.ncbi.nlm.nih.gov/pmc/articles/PMC1479498/.

Kurzban, Robert, Peter DeScioli, and Erin O'Brien, "Audience Effects on Moralistic Punishment," *Evolution and Human Behavior* 28 (2007): pp. 75–84, https://static1.squarespace.com/static/5252b095e4b06da77026f5e5/t/528d1b75e4b0d60933d9c24b/1384979317610/audience-effects-on-moralistic-punishment.pdf.

Frank, Christina, "Saying Goodbye: Talking to Kids About Death," *Parents Magazine*, April 2008, http://www.parents.com/toddlers-preschoolers/development/social/talking-to-kids-about-death/.

Freud, Sigmund, *The Future of an Illusion*, reprint edition in *The Complete Psychological Works of Sigmund Freud* (New York: Norton, 1989).

Hobbes, Thomas, *Leviathan*, 1651.

"How to Talk to Kids About Death," Website for the Child Development Institute, https://childdevelopmentinfo.com/how-to-be-a-parent/communication/talk-to-kids-death/.

Kondo, Marie, *The Life-Changing Art of Tidying-Up: The Japanese Art of Decluttering and Organizing* (Berkeley, CA: Ten Speed Press, 2014).

Konstan, David, "Epicurus," *The Stanford Encyclopedia of Philosophy* (Summer 2014 Edition), ed. Edward N. Zalta, http://plato.stanford.edu/archives/sum2014/entries/epicurus/.

Krishnamurti, Jiddu, *Think on These Things*, reprint edition (New York: HarperOne, 1989).

Lerning, Linda, *A Field Guide to Happiness: What I Learned in Bhutan about Living, Loving, and Waking Up* (Carlsbad, CA: Hay House, Inc., 2014).

Lindsay, James A., *Dot, Dot, Dot: Infinity Plus God Equals Folly* (Fareham, UK: Onus Books, 2013).

Lindsay, James A., *Everybody Is Wrong About God* (Durham, NC: Pitchstone Publishing, 2015).

Livingstone, *Gordon, Too Soon Old, Too Late Smart: Thirty True Things You Need to Know Now* (Philadelphia: Da Capo, 2008).

Lucretius, *De Rerum Natura*, in *The Portable Atheist: Essential Readings for the Nonbeliever*, ed. Christopher Hitchens, (Philadelphia: Da Capo, 2007).

Markman, Art, "Why Other People Are the Key to Our Happiness," *Psychology Today*, 22 Jun 2014, https://www.psychologytoday.com/blog/ulterior-motives/201407/why-other-people-are-the-key-our-happiness.

Martin, Courtney E., "Zen and the Art of Dying Well," *New York Times*, 14 August 2015, http://opinionator.blogs.nytimes.com/2015/08/14/zen-and-the-art-of-dying-well/.

Marx, Karl, *A Contribution to the Critique of Hegel's Philosophy of the Right*, 1844.

Matthews, Dave, "Ants Marching," on the album *Under the Table and Dreaming*, RCA Records, 1995.

Maynard, Brittany, "My Right to Death with Dignity at 29," *CNN*, 7 October 2014, http://www.cnn.com/2014/10/07/opinion/maynard-assisted-suicide-cancer-dignity/.

Medew, "The Big Sleep," *Canberra Times*, 2016, http://www.canberratimes.com.au/interactive/2016/the-big-sleep/.

Mencken, H. L., "Memorial Service," in *The Portable Atheist: Essential Readings for the Nonbeliever*, ed. Christopher Hitchens, (Philadelphia: Da Capo, 2007).

Murray, Ken, "How Doctors Die," *Web*, 30 November 2011, http://www.zocalopublicsquare.org/2011/11/30/how-doctors-die/ideas/nexus/.

Murray, Ken, "A Fascinating Look at How Doctors Choose to Die, *Reader's Digest*, available on the Web at http://www.rd.com/health/conditions/how-doctors-choose-to-die/.

Murray, Ken, "Why Doctors Die Differently," *Wall Street Journal*, 25 February 2012, http://www.wsj.com/articles/SB 10001424052970203918304577243321242833962.

Oaklander, Mandy, "Doctors Die at Home, Not at the Hospital, More than the Rest of Us: Study," *TIME*, 19 January 2016, http://time.com/4185691/doctors-death-hospice/.

O'Keefe, Tim, "Epicurus" Internet Encyclopedia of Philosophy, Section: "Death," http://www.iep.utm.edu/epicur/#SH5g.

Olson, Eric T., "The Epicurean View of Death," https://www.shef.ac.uk/polopoly_fs/1.101703!/file/EpicView2.pdf.

O'Neill, Stephanie, "Knowing How Doctors Die Can Change End of Life Discussions," *NPR*, 6 July 2015, http://www.npr.org/sections/health-shots/2015/07/06/413691959/knowing-how-doctors-die-can-change-end-of-life-discussions.

O'Reilly, Matthew, "'Am I Dying?' The Honest Answer," TED Talk [video], filmed July 2014, http://www.ted.com/talks/matthew_o_reilly_am_i_dying_the_honest_answer.

Pinker, Stephen, *The Blank Slate: The Modern Denial of Human Nature* (New York: Penguin, 2003).

Profeta, Louis M., "I Know You Love Me—Now Let Me Die," on LinkedIn.com, 16 January 2016, https://www.linkedin.com/pulse/i-know-you-love-me-now-let-die-louis-m-profeta-md.

Rinpoche, Sogyal, *The Tibetan Book of Living and Dying*, reprint edition (New York: Harper Collins, 1994).

Rogers, Kenny, "The Gambler," on the album *The Gambler*, United Artists, 1978.

Rogers, Kenny, duet with Dolly Parton, "You Can't Make Old Friends," on the album *You Can't Make Old Friends*, Warner Brothers, 2013.

Rowling, J. K., *Harry Potter and the Goblet of Fire* (New York: Scholastic, 2002).

Sagan, Carl, "In the Valley of Shadow," *Parade*, 10 March 1996.

Sandstrom, Gillian M. and Elizabeth W. Dunn, "Social Interaction and Well-Being: The Surprising Power of Weak Ties," *Personality and Social Psychology Bulletin* 40, no. 7 (July 2014): pp. 910–922.

Sartre, Jean-Paul, "Exististentialism Is a Humanism," drawn from the lecture given in 1946. Available at https://www.marxists.org/reference/archive/sartre/works/exist/sartre.htm.

Shainberg, Lawrence, "Finding 'The Zone'," *New York Times Magazine*, 9 April 1989, http://www.nytimes.com/1989/04/09/magazine/finding-the-zone.html?pagewanted=all.

Sheehan, Myles N., "On Dying Well," *America Magazine*, 19 July 2000, http://americamagazine.org/issue/305/article/dying-well.

Shelley, Percy Bysshe, "Ozymandias," 1818.

Shermer, Michael, "Why Do Death-Row Inmates Speak of Love?" *Scientific American*, 1 June 2016, http://www.

scientificamerican.com/article/why-do-death-row-inmates-speak-of-love/.

Singer, Peter, *Animal Liberation* (New York: Ecco Press, 2001).

Song, Sora, "Are We Happier Facing Death," *TIME*, 30 October 2007, http://content.time.com/time/health/article/0,8599,1678129,00.html.

Spilka, B., J. D Spangler, M. P. Rea, and C. B. Nelson, "Religion and Death: The Clerical Perspective," *Journal of Religion and Health* 20, (1981): pp. 299–306.

"Talking to Children About Death," Hospicenet.org, http://www.hospicenet.org/html/talking.html.

Taylor, H., "Large Majorities of People Believe They Will Go to Heaven; Only One in Fifty Thinks They Will Go to Hell," The Harris Poll no. 41 (12 August 1998).

Thomson, Anderson J., Jr., *Why We Believe in God(s): A Concise Guide to the Science of Faith* (Durham, NC: Pitchstone Publishing, 2011).

Tolkien, J. R. R., *Lord of the Rings, Part 3: The Return of the King*, 1954.

Tolkien, J. R. R., *The Silmarillion*. 1977.

Tolstoy, Leo, *The Death of Ivan Ilyich*, 1886.

Ware, Bronnie, "Regrets of the Dying," 19 November 2009, http://bronnieware.com/regrets-of-the-dying/.

Ware, Bronnie, *The Top Five Regrets of the Dying: A Life Transformed by the Dearly Departing* (Carlsbad, CA: Hay House, 2012).

Weiner, Eric, "Bhutan's Dark Secret to Happiness," *BBC*, 8 April 2015, http://www.bbc.com/travel/story/20150408-bhutans-dark-secret-to-happiness.

Wilber, Ken, "Death, Rebirth, and Meditation," from *The Collected Works of Ken Wilbur*, Volume 4, accessed on the Web at https://www.integrallife.com/integral-post/death-rebirth-and-meditation.

Wilber, Ken, *Grace and Grit: Spirituality and Healing in the Life and Death of Treya Killam Wilber* (Boulder, CO: Shambhala, 2001).

Wilson, Emily, "How Doctors Die," Harvard Medical School News, 21 January 2016, http://hms.harvard.edu/news/how-doctors-die.

Wittgenstein, Ludwig, Tractatus Logico-Philosophicus available on the Web at http://www.gutenberg.org/files/5740/5740-pdf.pdf.

ABOUT THE AUTHOR

James A. Lindsay holds degrees in physics and mathematics, with a doctorate in the latter. His work has appeared in many outlets, including *TIME*, *Scientific American*, and *The Philosopher's Magazine*. His previous books include *Dot, Dot, Dot: Infinity Plus God Equals Folly* and *Everybody Is Wrong about God*.

I would love to believe that when I die I will live again, that some thinking, feeling, remembering part of me will continue. But much as I want to believe that, and despite the ancient and worldwide cultural traditions that assert an afterlife, I know of nothing to suggest that it is more than wishful thinking. The world is so exquisite with so much love and moral depth, that there is no reason to deceive ourselves with pretty stories for which there's little good evidence. Far better it seems to me, in our vulnerability, is to look death in the eye and to be grateful every day for the brief but magnificent opportunity that life provides.

—Carl Sagan, in *Parade* (March 10, 1996)